A History of
FAVERSHAM
& OARE CREEKS
and the
FAVERSHAM
NAVIGATION

Frank Taylor

Compiled by Richard Walsh

CHAFFCUTTER

Published by
CHAFFCUTTER BOOKS
39 Friars Road, Braughing, Ware, Hertfordshire SG11 2NN, England

in association with
THE SOCIETY FOR SAILING BARGE RESEARCH

First published 2002, reprinted 2002 & 2007

Title page pictures -
Top: The hulk of the *Toreador* in Sea Reach.
Top centre: The sailing barge *Pretoria* leaves Faversham laden, towed by *Noni II*.
Bottom centre: Andrew Osborne (L), Capt. Alf Wood (tug master), Percy Monk and daughter with
the last Faversham Navigation tug, *Noni II*.
Bottom: The sideways launch of *Fairweather V* from what was by this time Southern Shipbuilders,
previously Pollock's shipyard.

The Society for Spritsail Barge Research was established in 1963 by a band of enthusiasts concerned that the rapid decline and possible extinction of these splendid and historically significant craft would pass largely unrecorded. From the thousands of Thames sailing barges once plying the estuaries of the south-east and beyond, today just a handful survive in active commission, charter parties and business guests replacing the grain, cement and coal cargoes of yesteryear.

Now renamed The Society for Sailing Barge Research, reflecting a broadening interest in other allied types of craft, the Society organises walks, talks and exhibitions and publishes Topsail, a regular treasure chest of sailing barge history profusely illustrated with fascinating photographs of long lost craft and the ports they once served. In 2006 the Society established an archive of sailing barge documents and photographs and is actively acquiring individual items and collections for preservation and study. Members also receive a twice yearly newsletter which highlights the fortunes of those barges which survive, as well as providing further snippits of our maritime heritage as ongoing research yields yet more of that trade, a way of life which from origins going back hundreds, even thousands of years, ceased in 1970 when the *Cambria* carried her last freight under sail alone.

Membership enquiries to Margaret Blackburn,
Lords Bridge Toll House, Lordsbridge, Tilney cum Islington, King's Lynn,
Norfolk PE34 3BW

THE BRITISH LIBRARY CATALOGUING IN PUBLICATION DATA:
A CATALOGUE RECORD FOR THIS BOOK IS AVAILABLE FROM THE BRITISH LIBRARY

ISBN 0-9532422-3-4

Printed and bound by
Piggott Black Bear Limited, The Paddocks, Cherry Hinton Road, Cambridge CB1 8DH

Contents

Throughout the text names of vessels are shown in *italics*.

Whilst every care has been taken over the reproduction of photographs, there are some from poor quality originals which are included on account of their historical significance.

The author's model of the Hollowshore bargeyard featured in this publication has been passed to Barry Tester, the present yard owner, in the hope that those interested may, by prior arrangement, visit in order to see the yard as it once was.

The Author

Frank Taylor was born in Faversham in 1933 and was the son, grandson, great-grandson and great-great-grandson of seafarers. During his boyhood at the end of World War II all his spare time was spent on either the local sailing barges or on the Faversham Navigation tug. Directly after leaving school he was employed as mate on Cremer's barges and later, due to the rapid decline of the barge trade, went away deep sea for ten years. Between deep sea voyages he was frequently called upon by one or other of the Faversham barge masters to ship aboard for the odd freight if they were not able to get a permanent mate.

Whilst deep sea he met his future wife Freda who was 2nd cook and baker and they sailed together for some three years on the South and East Africa runs. In 1959 he came ashore and spent the next thirty years in the Kent Fire Brigade with a further five years in industrial fire training.

For many years he has owned and sailed a twenty-one foot boat which is presently kept on a mooring near the head of Oare Creek. His other hobby is maritime research and making models of the various craft which have come to light as a result of delving in the archives of places and organisations connected with his former home town and its surroundings.

Acknowledgments

I wish to thank the following people from whom I have received much assistance in the preparation of this account. In alphabetical order, I would first thank my good friend John Cotton, retired barge mate and master and later Faversham River Inspector for the Medway Ports Authority, for his help in making available much of the supporting data and many photographs from his personal collection. The late Dick Dadson took pictures of the Creek over many years and I much appreciate the help of Avis Dadson, his widow, in providing some for inclusion. Next thanks are to Andrew Osborne, a boyhood friend and one time Mayor of Faversham, who spent a lifetime associated with the Creek, for his help in reading over the drafts and offering advice. To Robin Partis, one time tug engineer and again a close boyhood friend, who can rightly claim to have a photographic memory to confirm dates and remind me of half forgotten detail.

Also thanks to Richard Walsh and other friends and fellow enthusiasts from The Society for Sailing Barge Research. They have provided the opportunity for my records and recollections to be set in print and to reach a much wider audience than would otherwise have been possible. I hope the resultant publication justifies their belief that here was a story well worth the telling.

Last but not least, I wish to thank my wife Freda, my daughter Heather and my eldest grand-daughter Natasha, for their patience in typing and re-typing the many drafts, especially after the initial typescript was accidentally wiped clean.

Frank Taylor
Ashford
2002

Introduction

For some considerable time efforts have been made to gather information about the maritime aspects of Faversham to provide an account of the port during its most important years. These began in the early 1840s and lasted until its gradual decline following the end of World War II.

No account of the port of Faversham would be complete without mention of the area of the East Swale which is situated between the mouth of Faversham Creek and the sea. Accordingly a pair of charts, which give the layout of the Creek and estuary, indicating many of the places and locations in this account, have been included in order that the reader may more easily identify their whereabouts.

Faversham, it must be admitted, is much smaller in size and less important than its close neighbouring ports of London and Rochester. The harbour of Whitstable which lies outside the confines of the East Swale, was for many years regarded as the great rival to Faversham, but it must be remembered that many of the Whitstable craft were in fact registered at Faversham.

Little has been recorded in this account about Whitstable as this has more than adequately been covered in the book 'Merchant Ships of Whitstable' by Wallace Harvey. Likewise the area west of the East Swale is covered by the twin publications by D.L.Sattin 'Just off the Swale' and 'Barge Building and Barge Builders of the Swale'. An earlier period has been fully recorded in the much detailed history of Faversham by Edward Jacob.

The research that has gone into this account is based largely on the writer's own experiences with Faversham Creek dating from the latter part of World War II up until the 1960s and through the individual memories of many men who worked in the area.

It is interesting to note that Faversham Town Council have three old charts preserved and displayed in the Mayor's Parlour. These charts are not to any definite scale. The first shows the layout of the upper reaches of the Creek dated 1590. The second, dated 1608, indicates the route of the Creek and includes the whole of the East Swale. The last, dated 1745, again shows the upper reaches of the Creek. These charts, if little else, confirm the names of certain areas and are important in as much as they ensure that such names are not lost or forgotten with the passage of time.

The earliest of the charts preserved by the Faversham Town Council is dated 1590, showing the bends in the upper reaches which became an impediment to the size of vessels able to use the Creek in later years.

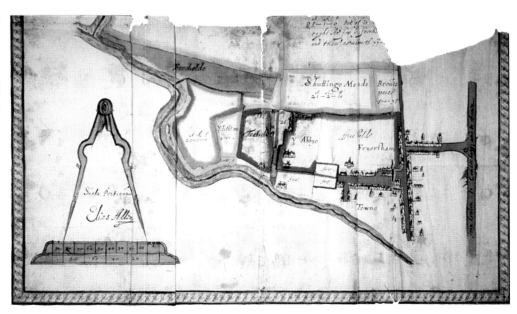

Right: Faversham Creek and East Swale chart dated 1608.

Centre Right: A Town of Faversham map dated 1745, showing the Creek and town in some detail. The horseshoe bow at the top right of the Creek was by-passed later.

Below: An aerial view of the northern part of the town with Faversham Creek and the East Swale beyond, taken around 1950. At the top left is seen the junction with Oare Creek at Hollowshore where the sheds of the Cremer barge yard still survive in company with the Shipwrights Arms pub. This remote hostelry, despite being less than 50 miles as the crow flies from Marble Arch, still has its own generator to provide lighting and power. The Faversham railway sidings at Iron Wharf are seen packed with trucks. Two sailing barges are just discernable, one at the Gasworks Quay to the bottom left of the photograph and the other, in the centre of the picture, at the lower end of Standard Quay.

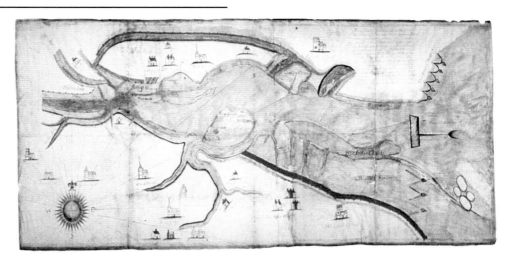

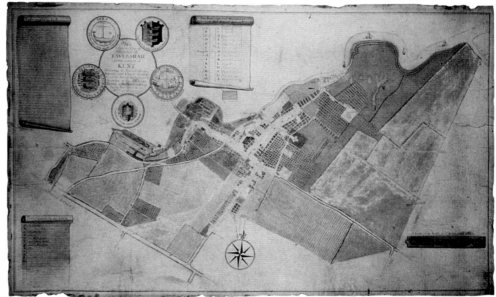

Chapter 1

The East Swale

The East Swale from time immemorial has been considered a safe anchorage for shipping in all winds other than strong blows from North East to a point South of East. Even in these wind directions, some shelter is possible if vessels penetrate further into the Swale and anchor above Harty Ferry on the island side, where the deepest part of the East Swale can be found.

Access into the East Swale from the sea is afforded at all states of the tide via the main channel which runs along the south side of the Columbine Spit and then passes between the Ham Gat and Pollard Spit buoys. When inward bound from the East, both these buoys and the low land of Shellness behind are often difficult to pick out.

Shellness - entrance to the East Swale

A second route into the East Swale from the north or from the Thames is over the Leysdown Flats, known to generations of Faversham men as the 'back of the land'. This route is via the Ham Gat, locally referred to as 'the M'. The Ham Gat has never been buoyed and for some years has had an unmarked wreck situated at its north east end. This channel should only be attempted on a rising tide from about half flood and certainly not later than half ebb. The 'back of the land' can be most unhealthy during strong winds.

Captain Bob Childs in his book 'Rochester Sailing Barges of the Victorian Era' records that during the night of 24th November 1864 the small barge *Earl of Macclesfield* with a freight of manure for Leysdown foundered in this area in bad weather. Her master, Captain William Jarrett, his wife and five of his children aged between 17 years

The East Swale seen from Harty Ferry

and 18 months were drowned. A further two sons, aged 12 years and 14 years, were saved by local Coastguards the next day after clinging to the rigging all night.

Captain Albert Keen of *James & Ann* has recorded an interesting account of the sinking of his barge. The barge struck the submerged wreckage of an aircraft, which had crashed during the then recently ended war. The wreckage penetrated the barge's bow causing her to sink. She was subsequently re-floated and the writer remembers her being towed into the Hollowshore barge yard for repair. This account is backed up by John Cotton who at that time was mate with Captain Charlie Ward in *Edith*. *Edith* was slightly ahead of *James & Ann* and managed to sail back to pick up *James & Ann*'s crew.

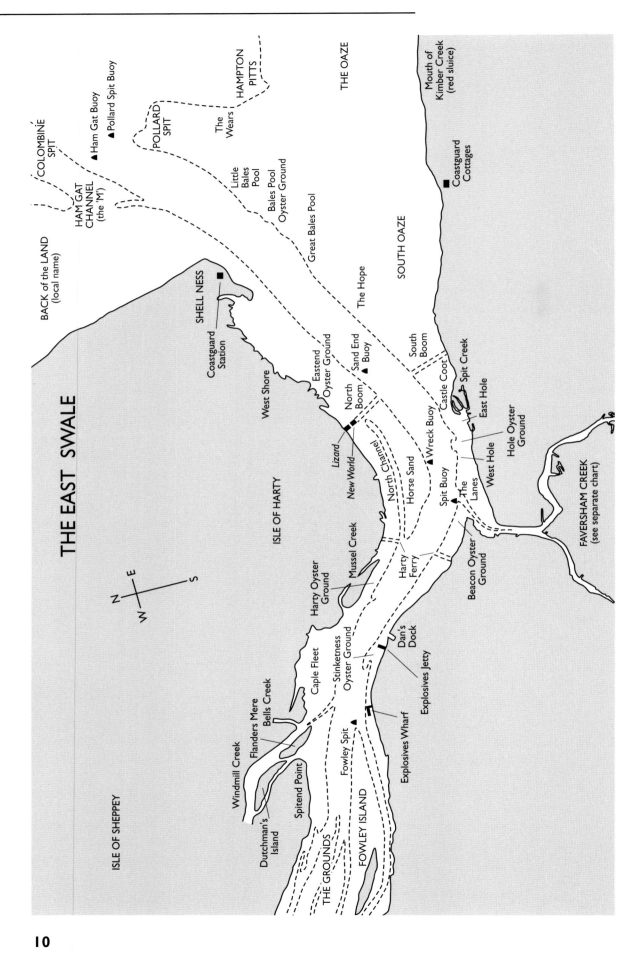

THE EAST SWALE

Let us look at the geography of the East Swale in some detail. The positions of the Faversham Oyster Company grounds are indicated on the chart. It would appear that there were seven separate grounds, namely Bales Pool, East End, Ness Ground, Stinket Ness, Harty Ground (58 acres), Beacon Ground (109 acres) and Hole Ground (175 acres). In about 1902 the Faversham Oyster Company found that three of their grounds, the Hole and Harty and to a lesser extent the Beacon Ground, were being polluted.

It was thought, and later proved, that the pollution was caused by the discharge of untreated sewage from Faversham. A complaint was made by the Oyster Company which resulted in an exchange of letters over a number of years. The Oyster Company finally served a writ. The writ resulted in a case heard in June 1908 at the High Court before Mr. Justice Eve. The hearing, which lasted some days, resulted in Faversham Corporation being found guilty of allowing untreated sewage to enter the Creek which in turn polluted the three oyster beds nearest to the entrance of Faversham Creek.

The Horse Sand is situated in the East Swale and is marked by the Sand End buoy and what is now called the Receptive buoy. The latter buoy was always known plainly as 'the wreck buoy' and was positioned to mark the wreck of a trawler that was blown up after hitting a mine during World War II. It would be interesting to know if the name of this Receptive buoy is that of the trawler that met her fate there. It is understood that the boiler from the trawler ended up on Fowley Island some miles to the west.

The Horse Sand was for years the traditional area where craft would be allowed to take the ground for a periodic scrub off. The sand is very firm and is the breeding ground for cockles. Before the advent of modern suction type cockle boats, the old type boats would appear from time to time and would put themselves on the sand and wait for the tide to drop. As soon as an individual boat was dry the crew would climb over the side and with the aid of wooden rakes and nets would harvest the live cockles which lie just below the surface of the sand. These cockles would be rinsed and carried back in baskets, or even on crude sledges, to be loaded aboard the cockle boats. When the tide made and the boats floated they would leave to return to their base, where the cockles would be boiled, riddled and marketed.

Towards the east end of the Horse Sand is the position of the old defence boom. The stumps of the piles of the south section of this boom can be plainly seen even today at low water. On the Sheppey side the hulks of the sailing barges *Lizard* and *New World* which were placed and sunk in their respective positions during the construction of the boom remain today. From the work book of the Faversham tug *Noni* the following entry in respect of the building of the boom may be of interest. 'Sunday September 3rd - War declared - Monday - 2 mooring wires brought to Harty to fix for boom defence - finished and left September 12th.' During much of World War II the boom closed off the East Swale and the route to or from Faversham Creek was via 'the grounds', Kings Ferry Bridge, the West Swale and Medway.

Before the Coastguard houses were constructed at Seasalter and Harty Ferry the Coastguard 'watch' were stationed afloat. Watch vessels during the period of this book were *Castle Coot* and *Cadmus*. The 120 ton *Castle Coot* was designated Watch Vessel No. 27 and was moored on the south shore due east of Faversham Creek. Named after an Irish castle her role was as base for the inspection of all craft arriving in the East Swale from the seaward, wherever bound. *Castle Coot* lent its name to the area of shell bank on the south shore, now part of a bird sanctuary. The other Watch Vessel was No. 24, *Cadmus*, stationed nearer to the mouth of Faversham Creek She was an ex. Naval brig, H.M.S. *Despatch*, over 100 feet long, with a crew of one officer and seven men, with their wives and families aboard. *Cadmus* had the job of checking craft using Faversham Creek, as well as providing assistance to craft in distress. Both craft were disposed of when the Coastguard accommodation was provided ashore.

Opposite: The Faversham sailing barge *Esther* in the East Swale in the early 1950s, with her master, Captain Percy Wildish and the mate, his son Dennis, retrieving the anchor. The tow rope is already set up and the tug *Noni II* waits to take her charge into the Creek.

Above right: Castle Coot to the east of Faversham Creek entrance.

Right: A series of buoys mark the entrance channel to Faversham Creek.

On the mainland side of the East Swale were sited a number of complexes involved in the manufacture of explosives. The remnants of the dock and wharves that served these works, both receiving raw materials and shipping away explosives, survive at the time of writing.

The Faversham Society have published a number of accounts on the Faversham explosives industry. During World War I one of the works was involved in a disastrous explosion which resulted in mass destruction and the death of more than 100 employees.

Remains of the explosives jetty at Stinket Ness. (Plan of jetty p.79)

The most westerly of these installations is just west of Stinket Ness where the piles of the explosive wharf remain. Just a few yards east of Stinket Ness is the ruin of the concrete and brick built explosives jetty. The remains of the rail track and pulley system employed to haul trucks to the end of this jetty are still apparent.

Approach to the explosives jetty east of Stinket Ness.

Head of the Stinket Ness explosives jetty.

The last installation along this stretch of the shoreline is sited even further eastward and is known as Dan's Dock. Many of the dock side timbers and piles of this large dock site are still in place and it was from here that Osborne Dan shipped bricks, flints and pottery. The odd barge was also built in this area. The last use of the dock was for explosives when I.C.I. took over the independent manufacturers.

Dan's Dock, which was latterly used for explosives shipments for I.C.I. in the 1930s. (Plan of dock p.79)

There is a record in the Faversham Navigation accounts of their dredger *Anchor* being contracted in 1938 and 1939 to undertake dredging of the dock.

The foreshore along this stretch is a barge graveyard and reference to 'The Last Berth of the Sailormen' published by the Society for Sailing Barge Research gives names of sailing barges hulked in the area. Between Dan's Dock and Harty Ferry for many years were the posts that indicated the measured half mile. Power driven craft built by James Pollock at Faversham used these marker posts to measure their speed. A number of runs, both with and against the tide, were undertaken to establish overall speed.

Chapter 2

Early Improvements

Let us first look at the various major improvements to Faversham creek that were made after 1840. Prior to 1840, it is understood that the administration of the creek was vested in the hands of the Faversham Town Council with financial assistance from the Trustees of the Hatch Charity. It would appear that a local businessman, Henry Hatch, who had lived in the 1500s had, on his death, left legacies which included a large amount of money, the interest from which was to benefit the town and port.

Examination of Faversham Navigation accounts from the mid 20th century indicate varying annual grants paid from this charity, ranging from £150 in 1926 up to £350 in 1968.

The Faversham Navigation Commission was formed in about 1843 to take over the day to day running of the port and came into being under the provisions of Acts of Parliament in 1842 and 1843. It would appear that the Commission had three standing members, namely the Mayor of Faversham, together with the Vicar of Faversham and the Chairman of Trustees of Public Charities. Added to these three were a number of others, being prominent town men. It is noted that in 1938 - 39 the Commissioners included Messrs. C.Cremer, H.S.Neame, F.Neame, S.J.Chambers, E.J.Fuller, A.Bax Chambers, T.J.Davies, E.E.Elgar and F.Cremer.

The Commissioners held quarterly meetings during January, April, July and October of each year with the Annual General Meeting being held on the second Tuesday of the month of February. On its formation, the Commissioners started off with some energy to improve the Creek fairway and to provide a tug to serve the Creek.

The initial improvements were, it is thought, to try to compete with its nearest neighbour Whitstable. It must be remembered that in about 1830, Whitstable had enjoyed the railway link from Canterbury which was a little later connected directly to the quays, making it the world's first rail linked harbour. Whitstable also had the advantage of direct access to and from the sea, whilst craft bound to Faversham had to enter the East Swale and negotiate the long winding Creek.

It is understood that the Commissioners had contacted Thomas Telford, the engineer, who came up with a plan to build a canal from Hollowshore to Powder Monkey Bay which was a sharp bend in the Creek not far from the present Iron Wharf. This canal was estimated to cost in the order of £32,000 and for unknown reasons was not proceeded with.

In 1842 a less ambitious scheme was approved which involved the by-pass of two bends

The New Cut around 1950, showing the lower part of the old course of the Creek clearly evident more than 100 years after the works were completed, as it still is today.

in the Creek, one at Powder Monkey Bay, mentioned above, and the other which was on the site of what was later to become Pollock's ship yard. This new project has always been referred to as the 'New Cut' and runs from a position near Chamber's Dock up to Crab Island near the end of the Front Brents. Other reaches including the 'S' bend at Nagden were deepened and straightened and where possible widened. The work started late in 1842 and took just over a year to complete and cost slightly more than that quoted for the canal project.

The New Cut, looking downstream from the lower end of Standard Quay in the late 1800s.

Chapter 3

Faversham Tugs

The first harbour master appointed by the Faversham Navigation is understood to have been Captain W. A. Chambers. Captain Chambers was authorised to hire a steam tug to serve the port, possibly initially on a trial basis. The paddle tug *Hercules* was duly hired. No details of this vessel's size and power can be traced, but it does appear the venture was a success.

In 1844, Captain Chambers was authorised to purchase a tug for Faversham but whilst a search was being made for suitable craft, the tug *Susannah* was hired from Tilbury owners for £8 per week. In April of the same year, a suitable vessel was located and the wooden paddle tug *Venus* was purchased for £400. She was 12 years old when purchased for work at Faversham, having been built at North Shields in 1832. She is recorded as measuring 58.4 feet by 10.4 feet by 6.4 feet with an engine rated at 16 N.H.P. *Venus* is said to have served Faversham for some 29 years, and it is recorded that following the completion of the New Cut she towed the fully laden 200 ton brig *Union* up to Standard Quay, which was no mean feat for *Union* was drawing eleven feet of water.

Memories must have been short or times hard, for many masters of craft would only 'take steam' when absolutely necessary. The published returns for one year, show *Venus* had an operating cost of £213.17s.2d. with a revenue of only £179.11s.10d., a loss of some £34.5s.4d. over the year.

With the passage of time, and despite 'losses' like this, it was decided to purchase a brand new tug and accordingly an order was placed with Messrs. Hepple & Co of North Shields. This replacement tug was the *Ajax* and she was delivered and entered service at Faversham in July 1862. Her master was Captain William Harris, the author's great, great grandfather. Her recorded dimensions were 57 feet by 14 feet which indicates that she was much the same size as *Venus*. No details are to hand as to her power or draft.

As has been stated, *Venus* was brought to Faversham in 1844 when she was 12 years old and it is claimed that she served the port for 29 years which would bring us up to 1873. It is recorded that *Ajax* was purchased new in 1862 which on the face of it would indicate that both *Venus* and *Ajax* worked together at Faversham for some 11 years. However this is most unlikely and accordingly it is suspected that *Venus* only served Faversham for some 18 years, though it is impossible to be certain.

Ajax was sold back to Hepple & Co. in 1883 after 21 years service, possibly in part exchange for the new tug *Pioneer* which is said to have cost some £3,400. *Pioneer* was rated at 40 N.H.P and measured 71 feet by 15.3 feet by 7.3 feet and served Faversham for well over 40 years, with Captain Harris as her master for many of her early years of service.

The Faversham Navigation paddle tug *Pioneer* seen here in an early livery, possibly shortly after arrival from her builders, towing a large ketch rigged barge and spritsail barge away from Faversham. Compare this picture with that on p.19 where she has a light coloured hull and funnel.

FAVERSHAM NAVIGATION.

RULES and REGULATIONS to be observed at the PORT of FAVERSHAM.

1.—That all Masters of Vessels requiring the Steam Tug shall, on arrival, report themselves to the Superintendent.

2.—That all Vessels, except Barges, shall be Towed in-turn, unless the Superintendent shall, from some special circumstance, consider it advisable to order otherwise.

3.—That all Vessels in Tow, stopping tide, or moored in the Creek, shall have their jib-boom rigged close in, the lower-yards tipped, top-sail-yards hoisted up, and braced fore and aft, studding-booms and irons taken off the yards, and while lying at the Quays, both anchors on board.

4.—That the Master or Owner of every Vessel shall give notice to the Superintendent of his requiring the Steam Tug to Tow them out, one tide at least previous to his being ready to be Towed.

5.—That the Commissioners of the Navigation shall not, under any circumstances, be responsible for damage done or received by any Vessel under Tow.

6.—That no Vessel drawing more than 11½ feet of Water, shall pass the Lower Sump without the permission of the Superintendent; and the Master and Owner of any Vessel breaking this Rule, will be held responsible for all damages arising from detention to other Vessels.

7.—That every Master or Person in charge of any Vessel shall, at the request of the Superintendent or his representative, move his Vessel, slack his ropes, or cause them to be slacked; and in case of his refusing to do so, his Vessel may be cast adrift, and he will be held responsible for all damage from detention or otherwise arising therefrom.

8.—That in any case in which a Vessel is moored by ropes from both sides of the Creek so as to obstruct the channel, a person shall be on Board at tide time to slack such ropes as may impede the Navigation; and, in case of neglect, the ropes may be cut, and the Master and Owner will be held responsible for any damage arising therefrom.

9.—That all Masters of Vessels shall, when required by the Superintendent so to do, produce their Certificates of Register.

10.—That the Masters or Owners of Vessels shall pay all Tolls or Dues before leaving the Port. The Superintendent is ordered strictly to enforce this Rule.

BY ORDER OF THE COMMISSIONERS,

JAMES TASSELL,
CLERK.

FAVERSHAM,
15th October, 1892.

Notices were often posted regarding the use of the Navigation. Here is illustrated the Port Rules and Regulations in force from 15th October 1892. Other notices concerning non-payment of dues and the consequences, as well as warnings regarding operation of the sluices and polluting the Navigation were among those displayed.

Pioneer around 1906, off the Town Quay towards the top of Faversham Creek. The manoevreability of a paddle tug had obvious advantages when working in the narrow upper reaches.

A finely detailed model of *Pioneer* made by the author.

Pioneer was scrapped in 1929 but no record can be found of where she finally ended her days or if she was owned elsewhere than at Faversham for the lost 3 years when the replacement tug came into service in 1926. It is suspected that *Pioneer* must have run at a big deficit during the latter part of her service. She had a crew of four, she was a coal burner and she must have incurred significant costs for repairs and maintenance due to her advancing years.

Although the writer has not been able to obtain details of the finances of the Faversham Navigation Commission, in the mid 1920s it is suspected that they were not very healthy, as the next tug to serve the port was hired. The replacement for *Pioneer* was *Noni* launched in February 1926 and delivered for service the following month.

Noni was the first of a total of eight tugs built at the Faversham yard of James Pollock & Sons for their *Lonie* class, their measurements being 54 feet by 13 feet by 5 feet. She was powered by a 120 B.H.P. Bolinder heavy oil engine which the maker claimed was equivalent to about 150 I.H.P. It has not so far

The tug *Noni* seen at work during the 1930s. The Faversham registered and owned sailing barge *James & Ann* lies alongside the quay, deep laden with timber, awaiting discharge. She was built at the nearby Conyer yard of Alfred White in 1903.

been possible to establish why the unusual name *Noni* was chosen. It could well have been derived from Pollock's chosen class name *Lonie*.

She was an ideal tug for Faversham with plenty of power at a reasonable draft and was in fact the first tug to be able to tow craft through the swing bridge into the pent or upper basin. All previous tugs at Faversham had been paddle tugs and the width of their sponsons had prohibited them from negotiating the bridge opening. (N.B. The recorded beam measurements of the paddle tugs exclude the width of the sponsons which would have added some 12 feet or more to the width of each tug).

The late Captain Lewis Wood who was, during his long career on the water, the master of many of Cremer's barges and also the father of Alf Wood who was the last tug master employed by Faversham Navigation, used to compare the changing times. Lew Wood was never a man to mince words and he always expounded his pet theory that "Barge masters have it easy now. In the old days Bill Harris would steam at a rate of knots up Brents Reach and when abreast of Whittle's yard, would slip the line of barges behind *Pioneer* to let them negotiate the bridge hole under their own way." He continued as a comparison "Nowadays, young Alf tows them right through and gently drops them off at their respective berth and even picks them up at the same berth for the outward tow."

The author's model of the first *Noni*.

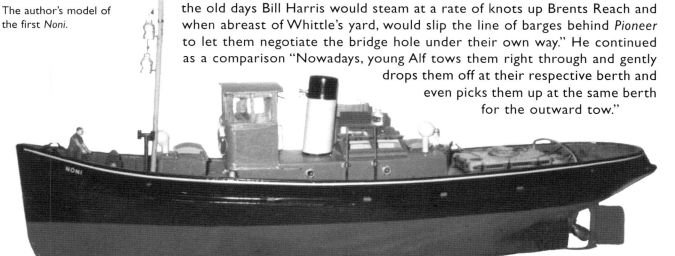

Noni was noted for her towing capability. An examination of her work book for the year 1938 indicated that she towed a line of five loaded barges on no less than eleven occasions in that year and indeed on 6th January 1938 she towed no less than 7 laden barges inward. These barges are listed as *York* (42 tons), *Berwick* (44 tons), *Ethel* (46 tons), *Bertie* (43 tons), *Wolsey* (65 tons), *Nellie* (43 tons) and *Magnet* (45 tons). This tow represented a combined total of 328 registered tons, carrying something approaching 1,000 tons of cargo. The length of her tow would have been well in excess of 700 feet. Alf Wood was master of *Noni* for much of her service at Faversham during the 1930s with Bert Cheeseman as engineer (later Albert Moon) and Charlie Jemmett as mate. Wages for her crew of 3 men ranged from £30 per quarter in 1926 up to about £60 per quarter in 1941. It is understood that *Noni* was never owned by the Faversham Navigation Commission who were said to be "too much in debt" at the time. Instead, she was owned by The Noni Syndicate Ltd which hired her to Faversham Navigation for £30 per month.

The motor tug *Noni* seen here with three laden barges inward bound for Faversham at the start of the 'S' bend in the late 1930s.

Noni served Faversham for more than 16 years until 12th April 1942 when she was requisitioned by the Admiralty for war service with the South Atlantic Command. She was delivered by her crew to Strood Pier on the Medway, to eventually be shipped as deck cargo to West Africa. After the war, she was re-named *Tunku* and served with the United Africa Company. It is understood that in 1947 she was sold to interests in Australia for more than she cost to build.

When *Noni* left Faversham in 1942, for the first time in almost 100 years, the port had no tug of their own and sailing craft were forced to depend on tows from power driven craft such as the *Stourgate* or one of the oil company tugs *Trustie* or *Audacitie*. As a stop gap measure in 1943, the Commissioners were able to acquire the services of a converted naval picket boat, the *Boy Mike* which the Noni Syndicate purchased from Dick Evenden, the Kings Ferry Bridge huffler (Pilot).

Boy Mike proved to be a poor replacement for *Noni*. According to Alf and Lew Wood, "She could not pull the skin off a rice pudding." However, she was fitted with twin rudders, set in line, and she would steer almost as well going astern as going ahead. She was small compared with some of the previous tugs, being only 46

feet long with a 9 foot beam. The engine was rated at 45 B.H.P., being a Parsons petrol/paraffin model. *Boy Mike* was disposed of after only 5 years service at Faversham and there followed a second short period when no tug was provided. Work books for *Boy Mike* indicate that on 26th February 1947 the sailing barges *East Anglia*, *M. Piper*, *Imperial*, *Sirdar* and *Magnet* all towed in loaded. Robin Partis, her former engineer/deck hand, remembers that this 5 barge tow was not possible for *Boy Mike* as she had insufficient power. As far as he is able to recall the tow on that day had to be split between the day and night tides for she found difficulty in towing even three loaded barges at once.

The converted Royal Navy picket boat *Boy Mike*, acquired when *Noni* was requisitioned for war service in 1942. She is seen here in Hollowshore Reach on the tug mooring. Access to the tug was possible at all states of the tide via the steps and dinghy moored on a continuous painter between the tug and shore.

During 1948 an ex-Admiralty Harbour Service Launch (H.S.L.) was purchased by the Noni Syndicate from Captain Shippick of the New Medway Steam Packet Company. She came into service at Faversham during the late summer and was named *Noni II* by her master, Alf Wood. *She* measured 52 feet by 13 feet by 5.5 feet and was powered by a 100 H.P Crossley Diesel. She was moored alongside Whittle's Wharf during the night of the 1953 floods. During that night she had floated onto the wharf and as the tide ebbed her keel caught the edge of the wharf and she leaned over outwards until she was floating on her beam ends, allowing water to pour into her after cabin and down her funnel to fill the engine room. She then fell off the wharf and was found at daylight laying on her starboard bilge on the creek bed. She was recovered, repaired and returned to service. *Noni II* served Faversham for just short of 8 years being sold to interests in Dover in 1956.

At the time of her disposal, although she had a book value of £1,113, she was sold for just £250. It was reported at

The sailing barge *Anglia* seen under tow deep laden in Hollowshore Reach around 1951 by the last of the Faversham Navigation tugs, the *Noni II*, which was sold in 1956.

the time that she had a broken engine crankshaft which it was estimated would cost in the order of £1,000 to replace. It is understood that the shaft was not replaced but was finally repaired by welding, though this failed again later. In 1973 *Noni II* was seen at Rye in very poor condition and it is believed that she was broken up and burned some two years later.

Noni II was the last of the Faversham Navigation tugs, and by 1968 the Faversham Navigation Commissioners had handed over control of the port to the Medway Ports Authority. The last cargo was handled in April 1989, towage until then, and since, undertaken by various privately owned 'tugs'.

Chapter 4

Silting and Pollution

The never ending task that faced the Navigation Commissioners was keeping the fairway of the Creek silt free. Situated within the Creek bridge opening are a set of sluice gates which hold the water within the Pent or basin. Just prior to low water sluices can be opened in these gates which allow the water in the pent to discharge with some force, which in turn scours silt from the bed of the Creek seaward. The scouring of the Creek immediately below the bridge on the Brents side had to be protected against erosion by the sluice. The bank outside the Coffee Tavern was reinforced with bundles of faggots which is understood to be a system practiced by the Dutch. The writer vividly remembers many times that he has assisted in replacement of withy beacons (needed to mark the channels), polling down the mud from Crab Island and riding the flow of released water down the creek to Nagden before the requirement to row became necessary.

Silt above the bridge in the Pent was shifted by small gangs of men working from a punt after the water had been released. These men luted loose silt from the sides of the Creek to the central stream which was finally flushed through the bridge opening with the aid of the fresh water sluices in Stonebridge Pond above the basin.

Above: The unusual triangular 'punt' in use above the swing bridge in the Pent. The gang of men are at work 'luting' mud from from the side of the Creek into the deepest part of the channel. The barge, moored to both banks, may have been put there to obstruct and, as a result, accelerate the flow of water when the Stonebridge pond fresh water sluices were opened to clear the silt.

Right: A warning notice from 1894 regarding the operation of the sluice.

FAVERSHAM NAVIGATION.

WORKING OF SLUICE.

Notice to Shipowners, Masters of Vessels and others.

When the Red Flag is hoisted at the Bridge it is to indicate that the Sluice will be worked the following tide.

To avoid damage all persons having charge of any vessel or other property upon the navigation, are hereby recommended to see the same is made secure.

The Commissioners do not, under any circumstances, hold themselves responsible for any damage that may be caused by the working of the Sluice.

By order of the Commissioners,

JAMES TASSELL, Clerk.

FAVERSHAM, May 12th, 1894.

W. Voile, Printer, and Stationer, Preston Street, Faversham.

The tranquil Stonebridge Pond was created to drive a mill which occupied a site just upstream from where the top of the basin now is. Although the mill started life grinding cereals, in the 1700s it was given over to the manufacture of gunpowder. Many buildings associated with the explosives works occupied the site, but following an explosion which took the lives of some workmen and also caused extensive damage to nearby buildings, much of the process was relocated further away from the town centre.

The opening of the sluice gates (as distinct from the sluice paddles) under the swing bridge tended to drag silt which built up between the pair of gates and the buttress of the bridge. This build up of silt, if left, tended to prevent the gates from being fully opened which in turn reduced the width of the bridge hole. One duty of the bridgeman was to clear this mud with the aid of the strange looking three sided mud punt which was moored adjacent to the upper side of the bridge house. There is an entry in the Navigation accounts for £100 being paid for dredging services during March 1936, despite the use of the sluice, and despite the passage of numerous craft using the Creek.

The fresh water sluices which hold back the water in Stonebridge Pond are now overgrown and neglected, but were once a vital part of the process of keeping the Creek clear of silt.

In about 1936, the Navigation Commissioners considered that a dredger was necessary and in the summer of 1937 they purchased the dredger barge *Anchor*. *Anchor* had been built at Queen's Ferry by Abdela & Mitchell Ltd for the firm of G.J.Binding & Sons who were sand, ballast and dredging contractors of Cardiff.

Anchor's details were length between perpendiculars 68 feet 7 inches, extreme beam 21 feet 3 inches and depth of hold 8 feet. She was rated at 99 GRT, 89 NRT and had a light draft of about 4 feet 9 inches. She was tiller steered. Her distinctive curved jib crane was powered by a coal burning steam engine mounted in the crane cab, which also drove her single screw propeller via a crown wheel and pinion. Her maximum speed with a fair tide was 3 or 4 knots.

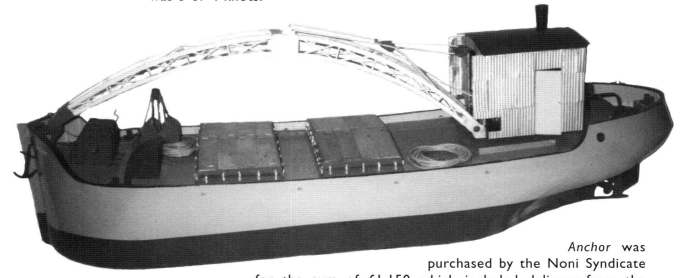

A fully working model of the coal burning steam dredger *Anchor* made by the author.

Anchor was purchased by the Noni Syndicate for the sum of £1,150 which included delivery from the Bristol Channel to Faversham. *Anchor* left Barry on 28th July 1937 in tow of the tug *Gaul* and was expected to arrive at Faversham on Saturday 30th or Sunday 31st July. *Anchor* was hired to the Faversham Navigation by the Noni Syndicate for £15 per month and was skippered by Charlie Dunning, an ex. barge mate previously with Cremer.

Research has indicated that *Anchor* was mainly employed dredging Faversham and Oare Creeks and the I.C.I. explosives docks and berths in the Swale. She also did work for other firms such as James Pollock and J.L.Eve Construction.

In mid 1940, *Anchor* was fitted out by Pollock for just short of £58 for work in Dover harbour and the towing firm of J.P.Knight were contracted for a further £177. 10s. 0d. for tending her whilst at Dover. In February 1941 the Faversham Navigation accounts show a sum of £1,541 headed "for total loss of *Anchor*". As late as 1949 a payment was made to Messrs. Mowll & Mowll, solicitors, of Dover for legal services headed "re. Crown Barge ANCHOR" (should read "Crane barge"?). A number of attempts have been made with Dover Harbour Board and others to find out the circumstances of her loss, but to no avail.

When reference was made to the Faversham Oyster Company in the section which covers the East Swale, mention was made of sewage pollution at the beginning of the 20th century. During the High Court action in June 1908, evidence was given that due to the trend within the town to construct water flushed toilets to replace the former earth toilets, liquid sewage was discharged into Faversham Creek. It was established in Court that sewage from the entire west area of the town was discharged into the pent above the creek swing bridge. The central area of the town discharged sewage via a number of pipes into Brents Reach whilst the eastern part of the town discharged sewage near the railway wharf (Iron wharf). This last discharge ran into Chambers' Dock which was considered by many at the time to be little more than an open sewer.

The description by witnesses of the state and condition of the Creek was that solid matter floated in large rafts in a brown liquid which was some 80% raw sewage, and that the smell, particularly in the hot weather, was very bad. The mind boggles at the thought of the old paddle tug *Pioneer* churning her way up through the mess described in Court.

Some evidence had been given by a barge master, Captain Henry Simmons, that 'rough stuff' and manure barges in Oare creek added to the general contamination when they pumped out their bilges. The Judge dismissed this as a very minor contribution to the pollution.

William Usher, the foreman shipwright at Hollowshore, also gave evidence that pollution could come from the many vessels at anchor in the East Swale that he had counted between the Sand End buoy and the mouth of the creek. This last evidence was rejected by Mr. Justice Eve, for in the Judge's opinion, these vessels had been counted four times per day and that the totals of these counts had given a grossly inflated grand total!

As previously stated, the Court found the case proven against Faversham Corporation and required them to pay damages to the Oyster Company and to take steps to prevent further pollution. It is understood that damages amounted to £4,250 plus costs, added to which was the cost of providing a new sewage treatment plant to overcome the problem.

The northern tip of Iron Wharf seen around 1938 from the north side of Chambers' Dock. Barges are discharging pit props for the Kentish coal mines. Although she was primarily intended for dredging, the *Anchor* is being utilised to assist with the unloading.

Chapter 5

Lower Reaches and Hollowshore

Having looked in some detail at the formation of the Faversham Navigation Commission together with its efforts to improve and maintain the efficient running of the port let us now take a look at the actual Creek itself.

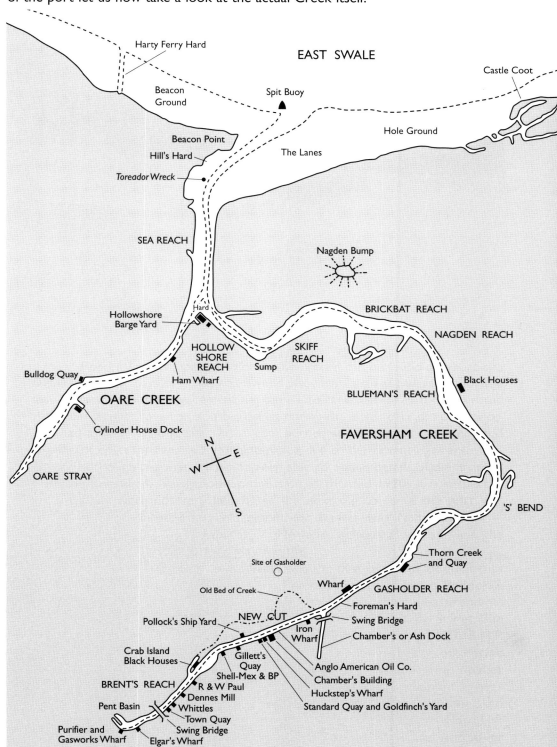

This plan of Oare and Faversham Creeks shows the tortuous route of the latter and the concentration of wharves in the upper reaches, many of which were within a stone's throw of the town centre.

It can be seen that the Creek spit runs out from Beacon Point for some distance into the East Swale. The end of the spit is today marked by a cardinal buoy which during the time under review was just a plain tarred wooden buoy. Faversham Navigation accounts show that for many years the Oyster Company maintained this buoy for the fee of £2 per year.

The eastern side of the fairway was always marked by withies. Just inside the Creek toward the west shore was known as Hill's Hard and Hill's Wharf. The hard was one of the traditional spots where fishermen and oystermen would service their boats and a store hut for this was situated on the sea wall. Hill's Wharf was used to receive coal cargoes from some of the larger brigs and schooners that were shipped in from the north. Some of the coal was destined for the Uplees explosive works whilst some was lightered away to Oare or Faversham.

Opposite top: Looking north from Hollowshore, during the Great Freeze of 1884. A variety of craft including tiller steered river barges and fishing boats are hemmed in the ice.

Right in the bight next to Hill's Hard are the remains of the old Brixham trawler *Toreador*. Some time just after World War II this craft was fitted out for a voyage to Australia. It is not recalled exactly what went wrong but she only managed to get from Ham Wharf to her final resting place. It is suspected that she took the ground and leaned the wrong way causing her to fall over and fill.

Past *Toreador*, we come to the first named reach of Faversham Creek, that is Sea Reach. The west side of this reach has traditionally been used for mooring fishing craft. The last of the old oyster smacks can still be seen on moorings here from time to time. She is the small smack *Emma* (FM22) originally owned by Frank 'Turp' Gregory, now in the hands of his son Jim. She dates from about 1850 and is some 24 feet in length. 'Turp' used to boast of the number of times that she had been 'doubled' in her life. It is remembered that at one time, after her sails were removed, she was fitted with a small Bolinder engine.

Half way along this Reach the high level national grid cables cross the Creek. The writer can vividly remember the first time he passed under the wires just after their installation. There was much concern on board as the barge *Pretoria* approached, as to whether her mast would clear. It was reported later by the staff at the Hollowshore yard that if a further half height had been added to our mast head there would still have been ample clearance.

At the end of the Sea Reach we come to the entrance to Oare Creek. At this junction is situated Hollowshore barge yard. This barge building and repair yard is typical of many of the yards that at one time were situated on the upper reaches of Faversham creek.

The yard layout is the subject of a model reflecting typical scenes of activity between the two world wars, constructed by the author. Photographs which follow show the model and its buildings. The roofing of some individual buildings has been removed to show the internal layouts.

Opposite bottom: A similar picture at low tide over 100 years later. The commercial traffic has gone. The entrance to Oare Creek is marked by the channel leaving the Creek in the middle distance.

It is known that between the early part of the 1800s and 1900 barges and other craft were built here on the open sea wall with the only buildings being the blacksmith's forge and saw pit/mess hut. At the turn of the century the yard was taken over by the Cremer family who owned and operated a number of brick fields and ran a fleet of barges engaged in the dry cargo, flint and brick trades. Thus was created an enterprise which was to survive for well over half a century, Cremer building and operating sailing barges to their own account, the last such vessels to be owned in these waters. Most barges were built in the open until around this time. The yards able to build under cover were few. With the demolition of Glover's, later Samuel West's, shed at Gravesend to make way for the Port of London Authority headquarters building in the early 1990s, the Hollowshore yard building is one of the last surviving in Kent. At the time of writing other barge building sheds survive at Conyer, and at Paglesham and Mistley in Essex.

In 1901, Charles Cremer built *Bertie* and *Nellie* both of 43 tons. It has been learned from Percy Dadson, a shipwright who worked on both craft, that *Bertie* was built completely in the open and that before her launch the frame work and roof of the main shed was built over her. After her launch *Nellie* was completed under partial cover when some of the sides were boxed in. The following year (1902) *Pretoria,* which was slightly larger at 44 tons, was the first barge to be built there under full cover. She was also the last barge built at the yard.

A board with the name 'F & H Cremer - Barge Builders and Repairers' was fixed to the north face of the yard facing Faversham creek. The yard was in the hands of the Cremer family until the early 1960s with Miss Ethel Cremer being concerned with the yard management. After Cremer, the yard passed to Jack Joby, who also ran the adjacent Shipwrights Arms pub until taken over by Testers in whose hands they are today.

The Shipwrights Arms was at Hollowshore long before the present bargeyard sheds were constructed in 1901. The first floor balcony gave thirsty shipwrights a commanding view of the Creek and East Swale. A barge hull lies on the foreshore, probably used as a store by the fishing boats which were based there. Another barge is alongside in Oare Creek, without sails, probably there for repair.

After World War II, due to the decrease of the Cremer fleet of barges, permanent staff at the yard were down to three hands, namely Bill Gregory, foreman shipwright, Bill Timpson his assistant and Ted Fisher, ships smith. Crews of barges in for repair were employed by the yard on a daily basis.

Left to right, Ted Fisher, Bill Gregory, foreman shipwright, and Bill Timpson at the Hollowshore yard in 1946.

The writer became associated with the yard in 1945, after the war ended, when he spent much of his out of school time as unpaid hand on the Faversham tug and going away on Cremer's barges. It is recalled that many trips were made by bicycle at the request of one or other of the barge skippers to collect stores from the yard,

The author's model of the Hollowshore bargeyard when operated by F & H Cremer in its heyday.

such as lamp glasses and cones for navigation lights and any number of other items of working equipment for the barge fleet.

Miss Ethel Cremer kept the roll of red bunting for making Cremer's bobs in her own home situated on the south outskirts of the town at Upper St. Ann's road. It was always put about that the reason why Cremer bobs were plain red was because they were able to buy bunting cheaply by the mile and chop off six foot lengths at will.

If a barge was at the yard for her periodic refit, a number of volunteers would gather there to, for example, unbend sails ready to be loaded into one of Cremer's brick lorries to be transported to the Goldfinch sail loft at Whitstable for repair and dressing. Dressing was however, more usually done in the yard on open ground south of the dock. The trip to Whitstable was always carried out on a Saturday morning when the lorries were not engaged in the transportation of bricks. It was a comparatively clean job to unbend sails to take to Whitstable but it was a heavy task to haul a mainsail from the back of the lorry up to the first floor of the sail loft. The dirty part of this task was bending freshly dressed sails back on the barge when all hands would be plastered in sail dressing. The yard formula for mixing sail dressing was 2 parts red ochre and 1 part yellow ochre (water in first, then add ochre) and mix in fish oil last.

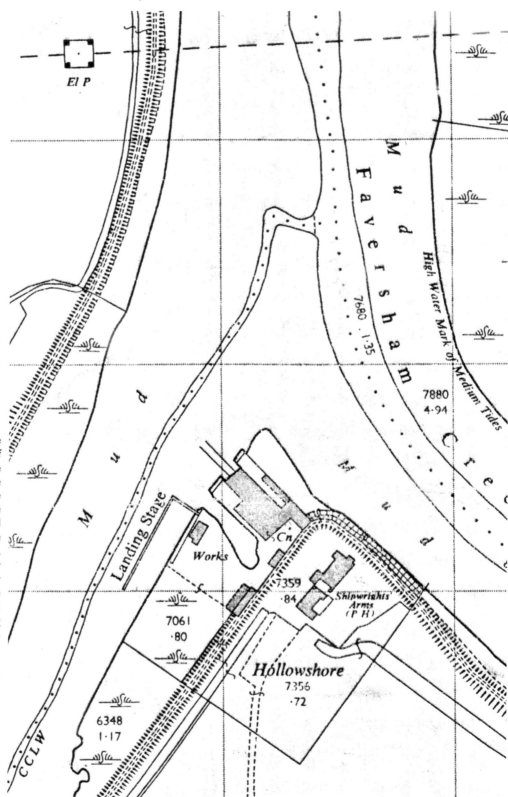

A plan of the Hollowshore area showing the junction of Faversham Creek with Oare Creek. Also to be noted is the detailed layout of the bargeyard premises with the main shed and slipway as well as the earlier buildings. The adjacent Shipwrights Arms was, and remains today, a very remote spot, presumably frequented in the past by those working at the yard, the local fishermen, the crews of visiting vessels awaiting their tide up one or other of the Creeks, and also perhaps quenching the thirst of workers from the nearby explosives factories.

Main Shed

The photograph shows the shed with the roof removed and the slip way with one of the local fishing smacks hauled up on the cradle to have a new stem fitted. A selection of shipwrights tools are modelled together with the hand turned grind stone in its water bath. This stone was used to sharpen the shipwrights adzes. The foreman's office is shown in the north east corner (top right) of the shed where 'valuables' such as brass screws, copper rivets and lamp glasses were stored. The shipwrights' tool bags were locked in here over the weekends.

Craft for repair would be floated onto the cradle between the barge blocks (not shown) in Oare creek and would be winched up into the shed with the aid of the massive hand operated winch in the yard near the gates to the sea wall. This winch was designed and built by Ted Fisher, although it is suspected that gears would have been obtained from the Faversham firm of Thomas Seager, iron founder. It was said that the winching up could take four men half a day. Above the main doors giving access to the creek there was a removable section in the gable end so as to clear a barge's stem and anchor windlass bitts.

Outside, the double ended 13' 6" boat shown in the area between the dock and the main shed (under a sail, bottom left) is a Water Wag named *Curlew* owned jointly by Robin Partis (tug engineer) and Andrew Osborne. She was one of a class of boat designed in the late 1880's by Thomas Middleton, originally for sailing in Kingston Harbour (now Dun Laoghaire) in the Irish Republic. The Water Wags claim to be the first international class as they were adopted by a surprising number of countries throughout the world. She is shown here during fitting out when half decks from salvaged wood were being fitted.

The author's model of the main shed at the Hollowshore yard. This shed is still in use for the repair and restoration of a variety of craft.

Engine Shed

The internal layout shows the Prince of Wales, one of the Cremer's old traction engines built at Rochester by Aveling & Porter, which had previously been used for hauling bricks at the firm's brickyards. The wheels had been removed and she was mounted on blocks. This engine was fired with off cuts of wood and was used to power the saw bench via a belt drive from the main fly wheel. A smaller drive wheel powered the heavy duty bench drill. This drill could be hand turned anti-clockwise when steam was not available.

The engine shed is situated between the main shed and the dock.

The engine was also used to supply steam to the steam chest shown on the south side (bottom right) outside the shed next to the dock. Barge's oak timbers such as wales and bow boards would be steamed in the chest which was sealed at either end with sacks for about 4 hours. When the foreman shipwright decided that the time was right the hot wood was drawn out, each man with rags to protect his bare hands, and whilst still hot, the timber would be bent and fixed into position. When worn out the Prince of Wales was replaced by a second traction engine which was not named.

A second use of this shed was for storage of rope and rigging, examples of which are shown on the long bench against the wall of the main shed. Also shown is Charlie Ward's Johnson Sea Horse 14hp outboard motor which for years was kept in the shed. Captain Charlie Ward was master and part owner of the sailing barge *Edith* which in 1928 was fitted with a second hand 4 cylinder Gleniffer petrol/paraffin auxiliary engine which came out of the hoy barge *Royal George*. Before the installation of this auxiliary engine, and also when his main engine was defective, Charlie used the outboard motor strapped to a leeboard to get him out of trouble, and for such as the last few twists and turns when *Edith'* was bound to Great Oakley Dock in Essex.

The same outboard was used after 1928 in the Cremer family yacht barge *Swiftsure* which spent the entire period of World War II laid up in Hollowshore Dock. Charlie Ward used to act as sailing master on *Swiftsure*.

Boat Shop and Faversham Navigation Hut

This shop was one of the original buildings on site and was in use before Cremer took over the yard, during the time when barges were built on the open sea wall. It was used for the construction of barge boats and for the manufacture of small work such as brick field barrows. Shown is a set of tools on the benches with a part built 14 foot barge boat. The old treadle lathe is on the left, just inside the door. The lathe was in the main used to turn up warping ends for mast case winches and handles for chaffcutter wheels.

In the late 1940s Bill Gregory would build a 14 foot clinker barge boat complete for just over £1 per foot.

The Faversham Navigation hut (partly seen in picture to right of boat shop, without roof removed) was always referred to as the "Olly shore 'ut". This hut was erected by the Navigation Commission as a store to be used by tug crews when the tug was on the nearby mooring. The hut's main use was to store bicycles, oars and small boat sails. A large pair of rubber thigh boots was kept in the hut for general use.

The shingle in the top left of the picture marks the Creek side, showing how close the buildings were to the water and highlighting the vantage point of the 'Olly shore 'ut'.

It had a good view north and eastwards towards the Swale and was regularly used as a shelter by Chris (surname not known), H. M. Customs sea wall patroller. When not in use the hut was kept locked shut but the 'chosen few' were aware that the key was kept in the gutter above the door on the left hand side!

Smith's Shop

The proximity of the smith's shop to the dock would help with the handling of the iron and steelwork.

This building, like the boat shop, pre-dated Cremer and was in the expert hands of Ted Fisher. Ted Fisher started his time as a ships smith working on sailing salvage vessels. Ted is shown in the model at work in the forge making up a mooring chain.

The anvil and hand operated bellows are included, the latter just behind the hearth. The 'striker' is shown standing in the corner. Strikers were normally the mate of any barge in for repair. On the bench are a set of tools to cut threads on the various large bolts that he made by hand and the cup of tallow used to lubricate when thread cutting.

Ted would make most of the iron work found on a barge such as mast bands, chain plates, cross trees, iron knees and bolts; in fact, all fittings with the exception of winches, chaffcutter wheels and the windlass, all of which being specialist iron castings, were bought in from Thomas Seager, the Faversham iron founder.

When striking for Ted, he always tapped the area to be struck with a small hammer for the striker to hit with the 14 pound hammer, when he would shout "don't tickle it - hit it". There was a block and tackle rigged to enable the leather bellows to be hoisted above high water mark in the event of big spring tides being predicted!

Mess Hut and Saw Pit

This is the last of the three pre-Cremer buildings. In this hut can be seen the wooden table with a bench down each side. The coal burning range complete with oven shown just inside the door was reputed to have come out of the *Swiftsure* built at Halling in 1876.

There were always set places in the hut for the three permanent staff. Bill Gregory occupied the seat in the north east corner with his back to the saw pit building. Bill Timpson would sit facing Bill while Ted Fisher sat next to Bill Timpson between him and the door. Visitors sat where they could.

The only 'cooking' done in the hut was cheese on toast which was made on most days, by placing a slice of bread with a chunk of cheese on it in the oven and letting the cheese melt to cover the bread. The hut was the meeting point for the barge crews when news was exchanged.

From time to time, Albert Keen of *James & Ann* would visit with his mate John Cotton, Percy Wildish with his son and mate Dennis of *Esther*, Charlie Frake from *Pretoria* with his mate George Waters and Charlie Ward of *Edith* and his mate Frank Taylor.

The mess hut was the accepted place of refuge during high spring tides. When the tide rose to flood the yard all hands would repair to the hut and would only leave when water came in over the threshold. Final evacuation to the sea wall via the main gate was the next stage, by when you expected to get wet after sloshing through thigh deep water. When the tide began to ebb the work started to retrieve timber or anything else likely to float away, and if there was a barge in the dock, it was vital to ensure that she settled back into the dock and did not sit on the dock side.

The saw pit can be seen behind the mess hut. Large baulks of timber were rolled over the pit on wooden rollers. The sawyer would work from a position on top of the log and his mate would work standing in the pit below the timber. The sawyer on top would push the two handed saw downward for the cutting stroke to the man below whose job was to push the saw back up again for the sawyer to make the next cutting stroke. In later years the saw pit was used for one off jobs or jobs too big to be handled by the steam saw, such as barge's stemposts.

To the left of the mess hut are the capping timbers of the dock; the engine shed is top left.

Paint Shop and Timber Store

The paint shop housed paint and tar used in the yard. The pair of large tubs on the floor were used to mix up the more frequently used paint such as 'mast colour' which is a light brown/buff colour. Over many years paint in these tubs had built up to form a coat of paint inside each tub more than 6 inches thick. From time to time the dried lead paint was scraped off, ground up and re-mixed for re-use.

The timber store (lean-to on paint shop) contained mostly crooks for knees and lengths of timber bought in for specific building or repair jobs.

The paint shop and timber store, far right, was in the south-east corner of the premises.

The Dock

Access into or out of the dock from Oare Creek was not possible for much more than an hour each side of high water during spring tides. With neap tides it was often touch and go if a barge floated on top of the tide.

The small windlass situated in front of the mess hut was often put to use to warp a barge into the dock. The windlass is said to have come out of the *Fanny*, an old swim headed barge built by Goldfinch at Faversham in about 1863.

Although there is still a dock in this location at the yard, the present structure is a large steel lighter which has been sunk in position and concreted in, with the creek end of the lighter removed to allow access.

The barge blocks in Oare Creek (not shown) were also said to have come out of the *Fanny* when she was broken up at the yard.

The barge shown is typical of one which had been newly re-launched from the main shed after doubling, and would then lie in the dock for re-fitting and rigging out. A replacement rudder has been shipped and new leeboards are shown in the yard. *Pretoria*'s were the last leeboards made at the yard.

A new 55 foot sprit is ashore on the south side of the dock where it has just been adzed out of a baulk of Oregon Pine and Ted Fisher has just finished the iron work for it.

The upturned boat represents one of Cremer's old barge boats long past its prime and by then owned by Albert (Rowdy) Ashby. The boat was used by Albert in his job as pilot for the many Dutch coasters bound to and from Faversham. It was mainly kept afloat by large amounts of tar plastered over numerous 'tingles' made out of old dried milk tins!

Cremer's *Atlas*, Faversham built in 1895, was in the fleet until World War II, following which she became a yacht barge, before retiring to a static houseboat role on the Thames at Shepperton. She sank on the weir above Chertsey in 1981 and was broken up. She is seen here in the Hollowshore dock whilst still in Cremer's ownership.

Bill Gregory's note book survives and records the following dimensions for the sailing barges under his care.

PRETORIA	Mast	31' from heel to underside of lower cap.
		6' 5" from bottom of lower cap to top of upper cap.
		37' 5" overall. Size of spar 11" x 10".
	Sprit	53' 2" between joggles (last made in 1938) Oregon Pine.
		$8^{3}/4$"lower end - 11" at sling - $8^{1}/2$" at upper end.
	Topmast	34' 2" hoist - 5' 6" pole - 3" move. (?)
	Lower cap	$7^{3}/4$" fore and aft - $7^{5}/8$" at hounds - $7^{3}/4$" at upper cap.
	Leeboards	17' long - 6' 6" fan. Square head plates 24" wide at fore end.
	Windlass welts	2' 10" long - $4^{3}/4$" inside underside.
ESTHER	Mast	36' 7" overall - 29' $10^{1}/2$" under lower cap $11^{1}/4$" square.
	Sprit	(replaced in 1938) 53' 5" between joggles - 11" at sling - 9" at lower end - $8^{1}/2$" at upper end.
	Topmast	36' 1" hoist - 5' 3" pole - caps $7^{1}/2$" - bar fid.
	Leeboards	16' 9" long - 7' fan - head plates 23" at smallest end.
JAMES & ANN	Mast	28' 2" from heel to bottom of lower cap.
		6' 7" from bottom of lower cap to top of upper cap 3" through upper cap 35' overall.
	Sprit	51' 0" between jogs. (August 1931)
		$9^{1}/2$" at bottom - $11^{1}/2$" at slings - $8^{1}/2$" at top.
	Topmast	33' hoist - 4' 6" pole - upper cap 7" lower cap $7^{1}/2$" square. Fitted with fid.
	Leeboards	18' long - 6' 6" fan - 2' 1" wide at head $3^{3}/4$" at head - $2^{3}/4$" at fan.

EDITH	Mast	32' 4" keel to lower cap and 8' mast head. 12" x 12" pitch pine.
	Topmast	36' 4¹/₂" hoist - 7' pole - Upper cap 8" - Lower cap 8" x 8"
		3" move (?) Size of pole 5" at bottom - 3" at top.
	Sprit	Oregon pine - 54' between jogs - 9" ends - 11¹/₂" slings.
	Main horse	17' long - 6" spring
	Windlass welts	2' 8" long.
Barge Sweeps		Length 28' - length of blade 9' 6" - blade 7" wide at tip - top of blade 3" (⁷/₈" thick) top of round 3¹/₂" - length of round 5' 6" - largest part of square 4", size under handle 3" - length of handle 12¹/₂".
Light Boards		4' long 11" x 1". Chock on fore end 4¹/₂" x 2".
Main Horse		Position of main horse on any barge 2" further forward on port side than starboard.

North Yard

The north yard is hidden by Tester's sailing barge *Orinoco*. The boat shop has been extended and by the time of this photograph, probably late 1960s, was occupied by the Hollowshore Cruising Club.

This small area between the big shed and fishermen's hard contained an open fronted small store mainly containing boat building timber and was a lean-to along the north boundary fence. Just clear of the store was the portable one man toilet. The toilet was re-sited from time to time. The toilet box was bottomless and discharged directly onto the salting. The toilet would have been automatically flushed twice in twenty four hours on spring tides and not at all on neap tides!

The yard remains at the time of writing in the hands of the Tester family and caters almost exclusively for yachts, ex. fishing smacks and other pleasure craft. Barry Tester has rebuilt a number of gaff rigged traditional sailing craft, some of which are moored nearby.

From time to time a barge can still be seen at the yard for refit. Until her sale to Maldon owners in 2001, Tester's own 1925 Mistley built steel barge *Portlight* was maintained there, or at other times one of the handful of sailing barges now used as yachts or passenger charter barges based at Faversham. *Portlight* was skippered by Lawrance (Lawrie) Tester for many years. He was the only barge master competing in the annual barge races who was older than the craft under his command. During a lifetime involvement on the Thames, despite many racing successes with his barge around the coast, he had never won the coveted Championship of the London River. Never, that is, until the Millennium Match in 2000 when he sailed a magnificent race to secure the winner's silver chalice. Well into his eighties by then, sadly he did not live on to defend his title, but his lifelong ambition had at least been realised before he died.

From a fleet once numbering some thousands, just a couple of dozen of these stately craft survive in commission today.

Most of the buildings from the Cremer era still survive in this view of the yard in the 1970s. The Shipwrights Arms is clearly seen with steps leading from the pub to the top of the sea wall. The yard buildings have no such protection and have been inundated during exceptional tides on a number of occasions. Oare Creek is in the foreground, Faversham Creek to the top of the photograph.

Chapter 6

Oare Creek

Looking to the north-east down Oare Creek from Ham Wharf towards Hollowshore. A very high tide on 12th February 1938 has left one barge high and dry on the wharf. There are new repairs to her starboard quarter, possibly a result of the incident, as she awaits the next big tides to hopefully re-float her. One of the tramway waggons is seen on the wharf.

The barge *James & Ann* was once on the blocks in the Creek just off the Hollowshore main shed. Capt. Albert Keen, her master, decided that as the water had almost left Oare Creek the time was ripe to 'grope for flounders'. Off he went steadily walking up the hard base of the central stream of the Creek until when about halfway between the yard and Ham Wharf, to his great surprise and consternation he sank in a hole and went instantly from knee deep to waist deep. He had found one of the fresh water springs that were said to come up through the gravel in certain points of the Creek bed!

Up Oare Creek on the port hand we come to Ham Wharf. This wharf was a brick loading wharf and was once connected to the brick fields at the end of Ham Road by a tramway. Just after World War II the whole of Oare Creek was almost deserted. Long gone were the days when sailing barges could be found by their dozens in the creek unloading 'rough stuff' and manure and in turn loading bricks, flints and explosives.

Immediately after World War II Ham Wharf became the home of Duttson's *Iota* where she lay as a yacht barge. The writer remembers the time when *Iota* broke adrift from her mooring and swung at right angles across the creek. As the tide ebbed the barge took the mud at both bow and stern leaving

Right: The sailing barge *Iota*, built at nearby Conyer in 1898, was converted to a yacht in 1945. She is seen here under sail, flying the burgee of the Little Ship Club, when owned by the Duttson family and based at Ham Wharf. She moved to Old Windsor where eventually she became derelict, being broken up in 1981.

her mid-ship section unsupported. It was a well known fact that *Iota* during her conversion to a yacht barge had her main keelson removed. All the 'experts' who came down to the wharf to judge the situation were adamant that she would not come off and that her back would be broken. She did however float and went on to serve the Duttson family as a home for many more years. The east shore of the Creek, from Hollowshore to Ham Wharf and beyond, comprises mud berths for a wide variety of yachts, reached via timber stagings. Above Ham Wharf the ground between these berths and the sea wall accommodates a number of laid up craft. Until 2001 Ham Wharf was home to *Portlight* where she used to lie outside a converted steel lighter that acts as a dry dock.

At the slight kink in Oare Creek, which is just about midway to the navigable limit, on the starboard hand we come to the remains of Bull Dog Quay, a brick and flint wharf.

Around 1925, barges loading explosives and bringing raw material to the Curtis & Harvey works. The 'Cylinder House' is just out of the picture to the left. Horse drawn covered carts are seen by the stumpie barge near the mouth of the dock, whilst the two tramway waggons, also horse drawn, serve the nearest barge.

On the opposite bank of Oare Creek is the former Curtis and Harvey explosives dock with its rounded roof saltpetre store. This building is always referred to as the 'Cylinder House', though in fact the real Cylinder House was behind it, where charcoal was made from cordwood in cylinders. The dock is called Cylinder House Dock.

Hereabouts is the only stretch of stone retaining wall in either Oare or Faversham Creeks. This is a fine masonry construction and pre-dates the 'Cylinder House'. There was an explosives wharf built here before the opening of the adjacent Marsh Works in 1787. This was because the risks associated with vessels waiting for their tide loaded with gunpowder at the Ordnance Wharf, in the centre of Faversham, was deigned too dangerous by the Borough Council and the loading was transferred to Oare Creek.

A windless day at the top of Oare Creek around 1900, The barge on the right is the *G.A.M.C.* immortalised in the first barge book, Cyril Ionides' 'A Floating Home'. In the book the *G.A.M.C.* is called the *Will Arding* before her conversion and *Ark Royal* afterwards. Ionides purchased the *G.A.M.C.* in 1910 for £140 and spent a further £235 on a luxurious conversion before berthing her at Stambridge on the River Roach in Essex. Her small size (74 feet x 17 feet overall, minimum 4 feet 3 inches under side decks) bestowed a number of disadvantages in her role as a house-boat, including lack of headroom except in the hatchways. She was eventually broken up in 1951 above Maldon's Fullbridge on the River Chelmer.

Above the dock the fairway tends to run close to the east bank until the last few hundred yards of navigable water where it runs more or less in the middle to where it ends at the main road between Oare and Davington. This last stretch of the Creek was always known as Oare Stray and is the only named reach within Oare Creek. Before World War II brick wharves occupied both sides of Oare Stray with bricks arriving from inland fields by tramway. The light railway between Davington Station and the Uplees Explosive Works also passed the head of the creek.

The head of the Creek is today in the hands of Young Boats Marine Services and is used for pleasure boat moorings. The author keeps his present boat on a mooring on the west bank.

Oare Stray from the road at the head of the Creek around the turn of the last century. The barge on the extreme left is deep laden, that ahead of her lies empty with hatchways open having discharged, or possibly ready to receive, a cargo. Many barges can be seen in the background in the explosives dock, where the prominent 'Cylinder House' dominates the Creekside.

Below: A similar view some 100 years later with a miscellany of pleasure craft lining the banks of the Creek.

Chapter 7

Faversham Creek - Middle and Upper Reaches

Let us now return to Hollowshore and rejoin Faversham Creek. At the end of Sea Reach where Oare and Faversham Creek part company we turn into Hollowshore Reach. At the west end of the reach, due north of the barge yard is situated Hollowshore Hard. This hard in times past was in constant use by small boats tending the fishing fleet and also commercial craft at anchor in the Swale. A fleet of small lighters was at one time kept at the hard which were used to lighter cargo from larger sea going vessels anchored in Sea Reach to locations in Oare and Faversham Creeks.

There is access to the hard at almost all states of tide except possibly 1 hour each side of low water on spring tides. The hard also gives access to the Shipwrights Arms Public House for persons coming ashore or leaving by boat. The public house has been in the hands of many tenants over the years and has seen much alteration and adaption over that time.

Looking south across Faversham Creek at the Hollowshore Hard in the early 1890s, beyond which the Shipwrights Arms nestles at the bottom of the steps behind the sea wall.

Old Lew Wood had the pub some time between the wars and used to tell of the times that they used to open outside normal licensing hours. It is understood that at one time a man was employed to keep a look out to warn if police were seen on the tram road approach track. One morning Lew was outwitted when police hid in the adjacent barge yard and caught him red-handed for the out of hours sale of alcohol.

Midway along Hollowshore Reach were the Faversham Navigation tug moorings where the Faversham tug was often moored so that it could get an early start to pick craft up from the Swale for the tow to Faversham. The mooring comprised two buoys situated on the south side of the fairway so that the tug lay moored fore and aft.

Access to the tug from the sea wall was possible at all states of tide without having to wade through mud or water. The arrangement was that a wooden walk way some 10" - 12" above the salting ran between the sea wall and a flight of steps

that followed the downward contour of the creek bank. These steps terminated about
12 feet from where the inside gunwale of the tug would lay when she was fast on the
mooring. The space between the tug and the foot of the steps was bridged by the tug's
boat which was kept in position by an endless rope line rove through pulley blocks on
the gunwale of the tug and on the head of the steps ashore. At low water one just
stepped off the tug into the boat, walked the length of the boat before getting to the
steps. When tug and boat were afloat one stepped from the tug into the boat and
pulled the boat towards the shore with the aid of the endless line.

Looking north-west down
Hollowshore Reach at low
water from The Sump. The
Faversham Navigation tug
Noni II is on her mooring in
this picture taken around
1950.

A photograph of Skiff Reach
looking up Faversham Creek
from The Sump, in 2001.

At the east end of Hollowshore Reach we come to the area known as The
Sump. This area is the elbow of the bend where Hollowshore Reach joins Skiff
Reach. The action of the tides in this area are cutting away the salting along the
south bank of Hollow Shore Reach and building up the Sump area. The bones of the
Gregory's 36 ft oyster smack *Secret* (FM23) could once be seen at her last resting
place in the bight, but they have long since been covered by the mud. The initials FM
and/or the single initial F were used for the Faversham fishing fleet register.

For many years the writer kept his and a friend's boat together on a pair of
trot moorings in the sump. Access to the craft moored here was possible at about
half flood and half ebb, which included wading through calf deep mud!

It is understood that Skiff Reach is
named because the oystermen moored
their skiffs in the vicinity. Indeed there is a
footpath which runs between The Sump
and the Brents at Faversham over the
marsh still called Drudger's Walk. The path
has its own simple plank bridges over the
intersecting dykes and in the present day is
known to very few people.

In the north bight of Skiff Reach just
before the start of Brickbat Reach are the
remains of a once substantial timber piled
quay. No definite name can be found for
this quay or wharf although it is thought to
have been built as a farm wharf to export
and import agricultural needs for the farms
on Nagden and Graveney Marshes.

Looking up-stream from the top of Nagden Bump before it was excavated to provide material to raise the sea walls. In the foreground is Brickbat Reach and to the left Nagden Reach which becomes Blueman's Reach past the buildings on the left the Creek.

Brickbat Reach has no particular features other than the brick burrs which line the north bank, and from which it is thought to have gained its name. Directly north of Brickbat Reach stood at one time the hill known as Nagden Bump. It was a sizeable hillock that rose out of the surrounding marsh land and appeared to be man-made rather than natural. Many theories have been put forward as to the purpose of Nagden Bump. Some are convinced that it was an ancient burial site while others say that it was put up to form a refuge for animals when the sea breached the sea walls in the area. Both explanations are open to doubt. In the 1950's the entire bump was excavated so that its earth could be used to raise the level of the nearby sea walls and no human remains were found. With regard to the shelter theory for animals one has to ask why the builders of the bump would go to the height that it was, when a shallower refuge would have been just as good and indeed easier to build in a period when mechanical equipment was not available.

A recent picture taken around low water looking up Blueman's Reach to the start of the 'S' bend.

The start of the 'S' bend at the top of Blueman's Reach. The first *Noni* tows deep laden barges to Faversham.

After Brickbat Reach comes Nagden Reach which in turn runs into Blueman's Reach before the start of the great 'S' bend. The land features in both banks are not notable with the exception of the farm buildings on the east bank.

Where the modern houses and buildings now stand were once a row of two storey residential buildings, tarred over for weather protection, known as Nagden Black Houses to differentiate them from other similar buildings at Crab Island on the Brents (see p.55). This section of the Creek was always thought of as the most difficult to navigate by those unfamiliar with the area.

The tortuous channel through the 'S' bend is clearly seen in this low water picture taken looking downstream in 2001.

Once round the 'S' bend we come to what is left of the mouth of Thorn Creek which stands next to Thorn Quay. This old waterway has been blocked off by the sea wall which was built many years ago across its mouth, but the old route of the creek can still be seen where it runs inland.

This gutway off the Creek channel marks the position of the entrance to Thorn Creek.

Immediately upstream from Thorn Quay the Faversham sewer outfall enters the creek. As a result of the 1908 court case the Faversham Corporation were required to take steps to prevent the town's sewage from polluting the Swale oyster beds. The sewage works were the direct consequence of this case.

As we run out of the last of the 'S' bend we enter Gasholder Reach which derives its name from the fact that when the town gas works were built at the head of the creek the 'town's fathers' thought that there was a danger if the gas storage holder was sited in the vicinity of residential accommodation. The result was that the gas works and retort house were constructed at the head of the creek and the gas produced was piped down to a gasholder sited on the marsh almost opposite Chambers' Dock.

When it was realised that the feared risk to residents was unfounded the gas holder was re-sited to the works at the head of the creek. The foundations of the original gas holder can be found on the marsh and the remains of the wharf can be seen on the creek bank, north side. A little further upstream on the port hand of the Creek was Foreman's Hard, now lost under silt.

Below: Looking up Gasholder Reach. The sailing barge *Monitor* lies on Foreman's Hard to the left of this photograph taken around 1890. She was Faversham built by John Goldfinch at his King's Head yard in 1862. Gillett's *Two Brothers* and the *Emma* (right), sails set, drift down the Creek outward bound.

Just above Foreman's Hard we come to Chambers' Dock or Ash Dock as it was once called. Chambers' Dock was originally widened and deepened to serve the Abbey brickfield, when Cook's Ditch was diverted into it. Cook's Ditch rose by the Parish Church and at one time flowed via a corn mill on Standard Quay into the Creek. The entrance to the dock was originally spanned by a timber pedestrian swing bridge (see pictures on pages 26 and 49) which has been replaced with a very narrow lifting bridge.

Chambers' Dock taken from the swing bridge by the Creek before 1900. On the left are the Abbey Brick fields. The barge *Alice Laws* was first registered on 30th June 1878 and was by 1900 owned by Henry Chambers, Brunton Wharf Potteries, Limehouse.

Above Chambers' Dock and Gasholder Reach we run into the New Cut which was dug in 1842/43 to by-pass the bends in the natural course of the creek.

The south bank of the New Cut from Chambers' Dock onwards is called Iron Wharf and it was built by the railway company when the branch line was run to the Creekside, and was named in anticipation of local expansion in the iron trades, which never came to fruition. Iron Wharf is remembered for not being used a lot by commercial traffic, but more as a berth where craft laid up. For many years after World War II the sole occupant of the wharf was an old war time L.C.T. and the site became progressively more derelict.

Eventually the Iron Wharf Boatyard was established and has occupied the site for over a quarter of a century under the same ownership. The riverside berths are occupied by a wide variety of craft, either based there, or under restoration. A number of old railway wagons survive in use as store sheds, but they were brought to the site by road. Around the yard little, if any evidence of the railway sidings can be traced, the whole area filled with yachts and old working boats laid up ashore.

Three steamers lie alongside Iron Wharf around 1915, when the war effort probably sustained an increase in the level of activity in the Creek.

Between Iron Wharf and Chambers' 'Big Building' was the wharf operated by the Anglo-American Oil Company for the import of petroleum products. The oil company's tanker *Stourgate* traded regularly to the berth with imports. *Stourgate* was built and delivered from Pollock's Faversham yard in about 1924, being some 90 ft in length and powered by a Bolinder heavy oil engine. The sound of her 135 b.h.p. engine was distinctive and it is remember that at times she blew perfect smoke rings from her funnel. The products imported at this wharf were pumped some distance to the road depot near Abbey Fields. At times the relief tanker *Cub H* ran to the quay.

The Esso tanker *Stourgate* was Faversham built at Pollock's shipyard just a little further up the Creek from the wharf she served in trade.

A recent photograph of Chamber's 'Big Building' built to serve the needs of the import and export trade of the nearby wharves. Faded sign-writing proclaims the 'United Fertiliser Co.' at high level, and below can be seen 'Chambers Wharfingers'. It is now occupied as offices by an insurance company.

A railway siding ran from the Iron Wharf about half the distance to the Pent and served Standard Quay and a number of the wharves upstream. Although by the mid 1960s just small steam shunting engines marshalled the wagons, in earlier times grander locomotives, like the one seen on the wharf in this 1890's picture, graced the rails.

Next comes Chambers' 'Big Building' which was always a general purpose import and export warehouse. The first wharf above Chambers' was known as Hucksteps, which was formerly called Steam Boat Quay. This was for years the town wharf for the Faversham tugs during the time that paddle tugs were used. It is thought that this berth was chosen due to the fact that it was situated in a reasonably deep indentation protected by the Chambers' Wharf which projected out towards the fairway. This indentation gave protection to the outside paddle box housing of the tugs (see picture on p.16). The Faversham Navigation Harbour Master's Office was at one time sited here on Standard Quay.

The lovely schooner barge *Goldfinch* early on the morning of her launching in 1894. Named after her builder, she was regarded as his best work. She loaded 250 tons of cargo, and sported double topsails on her foremast. After trading for almost 40 years, it was a tribute to her construction that she was still strong enough to sail to the West Indies, where she worked in the island trades for Booker Brothers of London. She was hulked in 1947 when owned in New Amsterdam, Guyana, South America.

A little further upstream we come to the site of Goldfinch's yard off Standard Quay where many barges and schooners were built, the most famous of which was the ketch barge *Goldfinch* which ended her days in the West Indies. The craft built at this yard were constructed some way inland from the bank of the Creek, and when launched, a section of the railway track which ran along the quayside had to be removed to allow the sliding ways for the launch to be laid over the roadway.

Standard Quay connects directly with Gillett's Wharf, at the junction of which was sited the heavy duty hand operated Scotch derrick belonging to Pollock's shipyard. It was used to unload steel plate brought in by rail to be further transported to their yard on the other side of the creek by flat bed motor transport. Gillett's berth had soft mud which tended to make craft 'suck down' when the tide flowed.

The main petroleum depot of Shell-Mex and BP was situated just upstream of Gillett's Wharf directly opposite Pollock's shipyard. The two steam tugs *Trustie* and *Audacitie* were employed on a regular basis to tow in pairs the tank barges *Antiknock* (112 tons), *British Flame* (75 tons), *Rocklight* (83 tons) and *Leicester* (69 tons) from the Isle of Grain terminal to the Faversham Depot. The M.V. *Jorie* also worked to the same depot. Both steam tugs were later replaced by the larger twin screw motor tug *Temeritie*. Faversham's own tug *Noni* was employed as a stand-in to tow *Antiknock* from Port Victoria to Faversham over the summer

Looking upstream from the 'Big Building' around 1895. Sailmaker L. C. Dane's thatched loft can also be seen on the previous page. The barge hull seen here lies athwart the route of the Goldfinch yard launchings. The rail track to the left was lifted so that the newly built craft could be launched into the Creek.

Looking downstream, the sailing barge *Henry*, the bawley *Hilda Marjorie* and many other traditional craft occupy Standard Quay in the early years of the 21st century.

Looking upstream, the oil company tugs *Trustie* and *Audacitie* are berthed at the upper end of Standard Quay. The Shell-Mex and B.P. Depot has the M.V. *Jorie* discharging by the hose gantries. To the right of this photograph, taken just after the end of World War II, is the coaster *Goldlynx* in the final stages of fitting out, following her sideways launch from Pollock's shipyard into the Creek.

The *B.P. Haulier* leaves the Faversham depot outward bound as crowds gather for the launch of the trawler *Fairweather V*.

of 1939. One of the last tankers to serve this terminal was the Pollock built *B.P. Haulier*. This vessel was unique to Faversham in as much that she was fitted with a Voith-Schneider 'propeller' unit and used to swing at the mouth of the Creek and come up to Faversham stern first, her length being just short of 150 ft. The terminal closed down on 30 April 1975.

On the other bank of the creek, directly opposite Gillett's Wharf and the petroleum depot, was Pollock's shipyard which had been built on the site of Perry's brickfield and White's Barge yard. Much of the area had been the previous bed of the creek before the New Cut was built. James Pollock, Sons & Co. Ltd. came to Faversham in about 1917 and among their first launchings were a pair of ferro-concrete coasters *Molliette* and *Violette* each of which were over 130 ft in length. The history of Pollock's yard is very well documented in the book by Anne Salmon entitled 'A Sideways Launch' published in 1992.

As we clear the upper end of the New Cut above Pollock's yard and the old Shell-Mex and B.P. Depot, we come to the widest part of the upper Creek. On the Brents side is the area once known as Crab Island with the abandoned part of the Creek bed, known as the Log Pond, behind. The tanker M.V. *Stourgate* used this part of the Creek to swing. When unloaded she would go up to Crab Island and ram her bows into the bank and go full ahead to turn. At the point she used for this manoeuvre was the foot path in front of the buildings known as the Black Cottages (not to be confused with the Nagden Black Houses). Over the years the sharp bows of *Stourgate,* and other power craft which used this area to swing, cut into the path which was periodically re-routed further inland. The Black Cottages were demolished some time after the 1953 floods.

There was a path which ran from the bridge which connected the Front Brents to Crab Island and which continued round the perimeter fence of the shipyard. Faversham Navigation had forced Pollock's to provide access through their boundary to maintain the tow path.

Before leaving the area of Crab Island one must make mention of the area known as Lew's Dock (unofficial name). Lewis Wood was a retired master of Cremer's barges and came out of their *Ethel* prior to the start of World

Looking downstream from Crab Island, Pollock's shipyard and the oil depot face each other across the Creek. In the foreground is the footpath and 'Lew's Dock' where the rowing boats are moored.

War II. He was also the father of Alf Wood, another ex. Cremer's barge master and later Faversham Navigation tug master (*Noni, Boy Mike, Noni II*).

Lew Wood was one of the finest men that one could ever hope to meet. Over the years, once young lads had proved themselves as being interested, Lew would ensure that each lad had a first class grounding in 'boatmanship'. Trainee lads would refer to Lew to his face as Mr Wood, but between themselves as 'Old Lew'.

The author distinctly remembers the time when he was about to purchase his first boat for £90, a not inconsiderable sum in those days. The post office had failed to send the £90 and the vendor was not prepared to let the boat go without cash in hand. My predicament became known to Lew who at once thrust £90 in cash into my hand, with no surety requested.

'Lew's dock' was situated on the starboard hand close to the upstream boundary of Pollock's yard. The dock comprised a small timber jetty built out from the tow path with a gate at the end, the jetty being only 3-4 feet long. Below the jetty was a small concrete lined dock just wide enough to take a barges boat, which would be moored so that its bows pointed out at right angles to the bank. It was only necessary to use the jetty to gain access to the boat at high water. Access at all other states of tide was via the concrete steps and path around the side of the jetty.

The boat, which was one of S.B. *Ethel's* cast-offs, was moored so that whilst sitting on the mud in her dock one only had to get aboard (dry foot), cast off lines and then, with the aid of a stout pole, cause the boat to be propelled down the mud. This was done by driving the pole vertically into the mud directly outside the transom of the boat. A short pull at the top of the pole had the effect of levering the boat a short distance forward in the soft mud. The process was repeated until either the momentum or slope of the mud bank took charge and the boat launched into the trickle of water in the middle of the creek. The man in charge of the swing bridge would, as pre-arranged with Lew, operate the sluices of the Pent gates and the resulting flood of water would take Lew's boat some two miles down stream with only a need to steer.

Capt. Lewis Wood (left) and his son Capt. Alf Wood, tug master, working on a boat at Crab Island Dock.

Although Lew Wood had no official authority in the running of the Creek during World War II and after, very little went on without his knowledge and prior 'approval'. Lew had many little sayings that people who had the honour and good fortune to know him will remember. When detailing 'his boys' to help in the erection of replacement withies to mark the channel he referred to this as "stomping in posties". He was also remembered for his favourite cure for all ills, 'oil of guaiacum', a popular remedy of the time, mixed with 'nitre, milk of sulphur and powdered rhubarb' and taken 'well stirred' with water.

On the opposite bank of the creek, immediately upstream of the Shell-Mex and BP oil jetty is the site of the former Shepherd's factory that made and shipped out Roman cement. At the turn of the last century it sold out to the A.P.C.M. (known to bargemen as 'The Combine') and not long after the premises were demolished to make way for a jam factory.

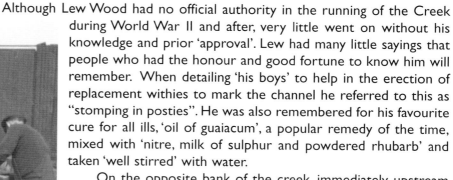

The cement works, founded by Shepherd, later passed into the ownership of Hilton, Anderson, Brooks & Co. before becoming part of the A.P.C.M. in the early 1900s. A small tiller steered topsail barge lies alongside the wharf and further up, a very much larger schooner has taken the ground in the middle of the Creek.

During the life of the writer the area has always been very untidy and it was here that the old steam tugs *Trustie* and *Audacitie* lay for some time awaiting their fate. Gerry More, an old freelance shipwright and handyman, often listed in the Faversham Navigation records for payment for work rendered, had a yard here at one time.

Whittle's timber yard had their log store on the other side of Belvedere Road just short of where the Creek railway branch ended.

Further upstream in Brents Reach, on the Front Brents are the rows of terraced houses that were the homes of many of the fishing families. Their boats would often be drawn up on the bank in front of their respective dwellings. The deep water channel is on the opposite side of the creek and accordingly only relatively small craft moored on the Brents side.

Looking downstream, on the north bank are the houses once occupied by the families of fishermen and others whose livelihoods were connected with the maritime activities of the Creek and beyond.

Looking downstream at the south bank in the 1960s. Trading under power alone, two of R & W Paul's ex. sailing barges are alongside their wharf. Nearer the camera the small coaster *Sigrid I* is being unloaded by the crane on Whittle's timber yard wharf.

The first wharf we come to on the Faversham side after the wilderness left by the demolished cement factory is that of R & W Paul. They were involved in the import and, to a much lesser extent, export by sea of grains and cereals. Paul's mostly used their own barges in this trade; they were always admired as being powerful well found craft. Anyone interested in further reference to the craft owned and operated by R & W Paul should read the book 'A Cross in the Topsail' by Roger Finch, published in 1979.

Directly next door to the mill of R & W Paul comes a second known as Dennes Mill. Unlike Paul who used their own craft, Dennes chartered in barges for their work. Cremer and Daniels Bros. did much of Dennes work. Dennes and to a lesser extent Gillett often sent grain cargoes away from Faversham by barge to destinations above London bridges. These away freights were usually just after the English harvest season.

Larger vessels did serve the Creek. This timber freight, probably from the Baltic, has arrived on a ship which will probably have to leave stern first.

The berth alongside Dennes was level with a solid base. The tug *Noni II* had her propeller removed and her stern gland adjusted here at low water, which saved time and money by not going into dock.

Adjacent to Dennes is the long wharf of Whittle's timber yard. Whittle had imported soft wood for many years, mainly from the Baltic. Faversham photographer Theo. Barber's pictures show square rigged sailing ships alongside, discharging the timber that they had carried direct. The later imports of timber were mainly carried on deep sea ships to London and then transhipped by sailing barge to Faversham. It was always understood that the sailing barge *Atlas*, although under Cremer's management, was partially owned by Whittle.

This wharf was also the last town mooring for the Faversham tugs after they changed from paddle to screw driven craft. Care had to be taken here to ensure that during high spring tides the tug did not float onto or become hung up on the wharf. To prevent this, large fender poles, some 6-8 feet above the edge of wharf, were fixed to the tugs berth. Steps were always taken to ballast the side of the tug nearest to the quay so that when she took the ground she leaned against the wharf rather than away from it, which might cause her to topple over.

The dangers of spring tides are all too evident in this photograph of an unidentified barge which got it's chine caught on the Town Quay at high water on October 9th 1904.

This picture taken around 1895 shows a schooner on the timber wharf and a ketch alongside the Town Quay in the distance. Beyond, the spritsail rig of a number of barges can be seen in the Pent above the swing bridge. The barge nearest the camera is the *Tyne*, probably that built at East Cowes in 1883.

The last open wharf on the Faversham bank before the Creek swing bridge is the Faversham Town Wharf. The old timber framed building at the back of the wharf has had many changes of use over the ages. It is understood that it may have started life as a warehouse, but in more recent times was a sailmakers loft under Alf Lott until its present use as an HQ for the local Sea Cadets (T.S. Hazard).

We now come to the swing bridge. Prior to 1881 the bridge which spanned the Creek was only 3'6" in width between handrails and consisted of a light iron platform carried on a pair of large iron girders. These girders were on the town side of the opening and were carried on four flanged wheels which ran on rails. When the bridge was required to be opened to allow the passage of craft through to the upper basin, a crab winch was operated to slide the bridge toward the Faversham side.

The swing bridge installed in 1881 is still in use to carry traffic, but is seldom, if ever opened. The mitre gates which retained the water are clearly seen. Craft would enter around the top of the tide when the water inside and out was at a similar height. A combination of the gate 'paddles' and the fresh water pond sluices at the top of the 'dock' were used to control the water level.

In 1881 this sliding bridge was replaced with a swing bridge which afforded a 7 foot wide roadway with a 3 foot wide path on both sides. The cost of the new swing bridge in 1881 was in the order of £1,385 exclusive of the cost of a temporary bridge and the approach roadway. The weight restriction placed on the bridge when built was 'not to exceed 12 tons'.

On the Faversham side of the bridge is the white painted pump house which supplies the hydraulic pressure to raise the bridge slightly to enable it to pivot. The mechanism for raising the bridge comprises a large hydraulic ram topped by a heavy iron weight, which is estimated to equal the total weight of the bridge. The weight and ram are raised with the aid of a hand operated rotary pump. The operation of a valve in the pump house will allow the weight to fall and at the same time hydraulically lift the bridge. In theory very simple but in practice not quite so. Over many years of use the efficiency of the equipment had deteriorated so that the weight had to be wedged in its up position with the aid of a cut down railway sleeper. Just prior to operation a few turns on the rotary pump were necessary to raise the weight to enable the timber prop to be removed. To lift up the weight from scratch required considerable effort on the rotary pump.

Around high water, one of Crescent Shipping's small coasters leaves the Pent in the mid-sixties, having just delivered her cargo.

Hootact was Dutch built as the *Gesina* in 1950 and was already twenty years old before joining the fleet of Medway based R Lapthorn & Co. Ltd. in 1970 and was nine years in their ownership. Here she is seen entering the Faversham basin through the swing bridge.

Below: Cremer's 1877 built *Providence* lies at the Shepherd Neame wharf deep laden. On the Brents side (left) the *Princess Royal*, built at Lambeth in 1856, appears under refit. She had by the time of this picture, taken around 1905, already passed into Dan's ownership, his bargeyard situated here in the Pent.

On the opposite side of the road is the small brick built bridge house. This building had a coal burning stove inside and was the general meeting place on Saturday mornings prior to the pubs opening. It has been known for as many as 10 bargemen to be crowded into an area not much more than 6 feet by 8 feet. All would be smoking pipes and come pub opening time the air was so thick it could be cut with a knife. This bridge house was built by E. Fuller & Sons in 1934 at a cost of £93.10s.11d. to replace a timber built structure which had burnt down. The brick built harbour office is situated on the Brents side of the bridge.

Hinged gates were provided across the road way at the Brents side to keep the public back when the bridge was open. The barrier on the Faversham side was less important, because the bridgeman remained on this side. This barrier was only a length of chain with a piece of red bunting tied in the centre. The actual swinging of the bridge once it had been hydraulically lifted was with the aid of blocks and wire, hauled by an old ex barge's crab winch situated outside the pump house. Heavy weights were sometimes necessary and were placed at opposite ends of the bridge to achieve a balance!

The hinged sluice gates in the bridge opening were opened with the aid of capstans mounted on each abutment. A concrete apron is constructed between the abutments beneath the gates. The release paddles, which were pivoted at low level at the base of each gate, were operated by a mechanism situated on the top of the gates.

In the early years after World War II Charlie Dunning, the Bridgeman, ex. master of the Faversham dredger *Anchor*, was operating the sluice and was knocked into the released water and drowned.

Tide tables, and a list of tolls and dues were displayed in the front window of the Harbour Office and a large board with a list of charges was displayed on the side of the pump house. A very tatty copy of a list of charges for 1938-39 has been examined and discernable extracts from this are recorded here.

A 1920s photograph taken from the top of one of the gasholders, of the wharves on the Faversham side of the Pent. Alongside the fertiliser wharf is the *C.I.V.* which ultimately became a yacht barge in 1964, but was derelict by 1980. Outside her is the *Aberdeen*, Both craft were in the ownership of the Sittingbourne brick-maker and barge builder, Wills & Packham, the *C.I.V.* built by them in 1901.

Tolls on coal		- 6d per ton
Harbour dues		- 5d per reg. ton for vessels 10 tons and upwards
		- 3d per reg. ton for vessels below 10 tons
Towage	(sea-going)	- 7d per reg. ton loaded - 5d per ton light
		No single craft towed for less than £1.10s.0d
	(River barges)	- 4^{1}/2d per reg. ton loaded - 3^{1}/2d per ton light
		No single barge towed for less than £1
Oare Creek towage		- 3d per reg. ton - in or out
		No single barge towed for less than £1

The first wharf on the Faversham side above the bridge is Shepherd Neame's brewery wharf, now built over to form a bottling plant.

On the Brents shore immediately above the bridge are the piles of the former Co-op coal wharf. Further up on the same side was situated Dan's barge building yard which after closing was replaced with a roller skating rink, which later burned down.

The last wharf on this side was Ordnance Wharf. Here explosives were once loaded from the gunpowder mills situated at the end of the fresh water Stonebridge Pond. The sluices from these mills are still in place and were used to flush sludge from the middle of the upper basin at low water.

On the Faversham side of the basin after Shepherd Neame comes a wharf which has been put to a wide variety of uses. At one time it was operated as a coal wharf by the firm of Francis Davis whose other interest was transport and road haulage.

The next wharf was occupied by the fertiliser importer Elgar which was later known as Agrigano. After World War II much fertiliser was brought to this wharf by Dutch coasters direct from the continent. Local sailing barges were also employed in the transportation of fertiliser from the London docks. The firm had very efficient unloading equipment in the form of an electrically operated overhead crane backed up by motorised mobile Coles cranes.

The last wharf is situated on the Faversham side and is called Gas Works Wharf. This wharf was possibly the most used import wharf on the creek as it is estimated that 250-300 tons of gas works coal would have unloaded here every week.

The Gas Works Wharf also includes the smaller Purifier Wharf which sticks out like a small finger parallel to the main wharf. The Faversham Freightage Co., formerly F & H Cremer, had the main contract to bring gas coal from London to Faversham. After the end of World War II, except during adverse winds, it was usual to see at least two of Cremer's coal laden sailing barges above the bridge, one alongside the crane and the second awaiting her turn. The writer can recall that in 1949 the rates paid to bring gas coal from Erith to Faversham was 6/6d per ton, my share as mate being 1/1d per ton.

Coal was grabbed out of the barge's hold by the old steam crane and grab mounted on the wharf. The coal was discharged into a raised hopper used to fill wheeled tipper trucks which were pushed by hand into the works. Barges were unloaded by first working out the main hold, which left a half unloaded barge well down by the head. This was standard practice when unloading sailing barges, so that when they took the ground on the ebb tide, their bows touched first so that they did not damage their rudders.

The gas works berth had soft mud and if a loaded barge had settled on the mud after the sluice had been run, she would sometimes be held down by suction. Often this suction held the barge until there was water over her deck.

63

Many barge masters said that the best way to break the suction was to climb the mast and to strike the main masthead cap with a maul. This would break the suction by the shock wave and let the barge rise. This was never witnessed by the author who only ever saw less dramatic methods, such as looping a chain down one side of the barge, under the flat bottom and up the other side. This method was used when warning was given that the sluice was to be run. A sharp sawing motion on the chain allowed water to get under the bottom and thus break the suction. The rising motion of the barges was at times very violent, for they would rarely lift on an even keel.

The *Lyford Anna* was one of the many yacht barge conversions done by the Whitewall Barge, Yacht and Boat Company around 1950. In trade she was the *Cereal*, famous for capsizing when entering Whitstable in 1929. In this photograph taken in the 1990s, she is abandoned sunk at the equally derelict Purifier Wharf at the top of the Pent. She was broken up shortly after.

Chapter 8

People and Barges of Faversham Creek

Having covered the topography of Faversham Creek let us now turn to people and uses of the Creek that have not been covered in the preceding account. Until relatively recent years the prosperity of the town was largely dependent on the success of the businesses that relied on the Creek for their trade. In some instances this was for the supply of raw materials, in others the shipping of goods to their markets. Much of this activity was based on the products of the area's brick and cement industry as well as the agriculture of the locality and the business of the local shipyards. Inevitably businesses and organisations which serviced these needs via the Creek were also important employers.

The importance of the Creek and its surroundings was recognised by a significant proportion of the community, many of whom would have had family and friends reliant for their income on jobs connected with the Creek. This importance showed itself in the large numbers who would turn out to watch the launch of a new vessel from the yards on the Creeksides.

Crowds grabbed every vantage point for a launch, on this occasion from Pollock's yard opposite these barges alongside Standard Quay. In the foreground Gillett's *Ella*, Faversham built in 1874, appears unrigged. She was derelict in Shepherd's Creek in the West Swale by 1939.

Faversham had a combined H.M. Customs and Mercantile Marine Office for some years. Before World War II this office was situated at 15 East Street, Faversham and, during the period that the writer can personally recall, was in the charge of Roy Francombe. At the beginning of World War II the office and Roy moved to an address in Stone Street, Faversham. Mr Francombe would call at the bridge house when one of the many Dutch coasters were due to pass through the swing bridge, before he proceeded to Elgar's Wharf to clear the individual vessels.

There was also a Customs officer named Chris who was attached to the establishment and whose duty it was to patrol the sea walls of both the Creek and Swale at odd times during day and night. Often Chris would be encountered trudging along the bleak sea wall, pushing his bicycle, whilst on patrol.

Cremer's *Bertie* after her conversion to a yacht-barge, seen here in 1948 moored outside The Crabshell pub in Salcombe, Devon.

The writer still has old Seamen's Books and certificates of discharge issued to both himself and to his late father by the Faversham Mercantile Marine Office, when both were deep sea seamen.

The largest fleet of sailing barges owned at and working from Faversham was that owned by the Cremer family. The firm's name after World War II was changed to the Faversham Freightage Company. In its hey-day, if memory is correct, the fleet just prior to World War II comprised no less than ten barges. The craft, listed in alphabetical order, were *Atlas*, *Bertie*, *Edith*, *Esther*, *Ethel*, *James & Ann*, *John & Mary*, *Magnet*, *Nellie* and *Pretoria*. By around the end of World War II the fleet was reduced from ten down to only four, these being *Edith*, *Esther*, *James & Ann* and *Pretoria*.

Cremer's *Edith* in the Wallet channel off the Essex coast, deep laden, heading towards Harwich on 13th July 1938.

The masters of the pre-war fleet were dominated by the Manual and Wood families. The Woods have already been referred to. Fred Manual, previously master of *Nellie* had left Cremer and had command of the big *Lord Churchill* owned by Cremer's associated firm Daniels Brothers (Whitstable) Limited. The other Manuals, James and 'Lightning' had both come ashore to work.

After World War II, *Edith*, considered to be the flagship, was under the command of Capt. Charlie Ward, *Esther* was with Capt. Percy Wildish, Capt. Albert Keen had the *James & Ann* and Capt. Charles Frake the *Pretoria*.

Cremer's *Pretoria*, when nearly new, was used like a yacht for summer trips and holidays. She is seen here flying a flag with C & Co. superimposed on the plain ground. Some form of temporary skylight appears fixed to the hatches. It can also be seen bottom left in the picture below.

Below: Under way on a holiday trip, with crew and passengers posed for a commemorative photograph aboard *Pretoria*. Those pictured are believed to include Charles Cremer at the back of the photograph holding the mizzen forestay, his sons Fred and Harry, back row left and right, and his daughters Ethel and Nellie who gave their names to two of the firm's barges which were built at their Hollowshore yard. The skipper at the wheel is thought to be Capt. Henry Simmons (see p.26).

Other masters known to the writer lived in Faversham. Capt. James Waters was master and owner of the big Faversham ketch barge *Goldfinch* built by Goldfinch at Faversham in 1894. Capt. Waters retired from the sea in the early 1930s and *Goldfinch* was sold away and sailed out to the West Indies to work for her new owners. Capt. Waters retired to Jutland House in Newton Road, Faversham, which was directly opposite the author's boyhood home.

Another ex-coasting master was Captain Harry Hoare who lived in Norman Road, Faversham. Capt. Hoare had been master of one of Samuel West's big coasting barges. Capt. Hoare did not have the look of a typical retired barge master as he always sported a soft grey trilby hat and walked with a silver topped cane!

Cremer's *Edith* when in Cary's ownership, racing on the Medway in the early 1900s.

The last four remaining Cremer sailing barges were always beautifully kept up and well maintained. The reader may be interested in more particulars of the final four Cremer craft and details of their ultimate fate.

Edith was built and launched in 1904 by Alfred White at Sittingbourne and registered at Rochester. Her Official Number was 118208 and she later had the signal letters MJDY allocated for wartime recognition by flag hoist. Her first owner after launch was C.L.Cary of the Sharps Green Cement Works on the Medway.

One of her original masters was Capt. T. Bolton. When new she was mahogany sheathed. She entered some of the Thames and Medway barge matches where she achieved some reasonable results, gaining 3rd place in the 1905 and 1906 Medway Barge Sailing Matches.

In 1913 she was purchased by Cremer and Captain Charlie Ward was master and part owner of her for the next 38 years, until Charlie retired at the age of 75 in 1950.

Around 1927/28 *Edith* was fitted with a new 4 cylinder Gleniffer petrol/paraffin auxiliary engine. This was removed in 1946 when she went back to full sail. When bought by Cremer her mahogany hull sheathing was removed.

Her principle particulars were; Length 85.5 feet, Beam 19.1 feet, Minimum height under deck 5.7 feet; 57 Reg. Tons, 70 Gross Tons - later 68 tons; cargo capacity 134 tons for river work as an auxiliary, 150 tons prior to engine installation.

After the retirement of Capt. Ward she was taken over by Captain Charles Frake and she was later fitted with a new engine and subsequently sold by Cremer. Her final resting place is as a hulk on the River Tamar.

Right: Captain Charlie Ward on board *Edith*.

Seen in the Faversham Pent around 1955, *Edith* is trading as a motor barge, by then flying the white 'D' on blue flag of Daniels Brothers (Whitstable) Limited.

Pretoria lies loaded in Whitstable Harbour on 17th July 1950.

Capt. Charlie Frake aboard *Edith* alongside *Esther*.

Pretoria as a yacht-barge (centre of picture) competes in the 52nd Medway race in 1960, a windless day resulting in probably the shortest course ever sailed, the winner in her class still taking 6 hours 24 minutes to finish.

Pretoria was the last of the trio of sailing barges built by Cremer at his Hollowshore yard for his own account. Her launch was in 1902 and her registration was at Faversham, Official Number 114458. She is believed to be the last but one sailing barge to be built at Faversham, though a number of barges were subsequently rebuilt there, including the 'ironpot' *Wyvenhoe* at Pollock's shortly after World War II.

She was a very good looking craft and as with all Cremer's fleet well maintained. Captain Charles Frake was her master for some years after World War II and under him she did some very fast trips. On more than one occasion she is recorded as leaving Faversham light on a day tide and returning from Erith for the next day tide with a full load of gas works coal, a round trip of some 24 hours.

Captain Frake always considered *Pretoria* to be weak and in need of bracing with tie bolts. It may be that this weakness could have been caused by the fact that her rigging was set up with bottle screws, instead of the more usual deadeyes and lanyards, and it was known that Captain Frake pressed *Pretoria* hard for her living.

Her principle particulars were: Length 80.1 feet, Beam 19 feet, Minimum height under deck 5.6 feet; 44 Reg. Tons, cargo capacity 119 tons for river work.

After coming out of trade she was a yacht barge for some years before becoming a restaurant on the Thames, permanently moored alongside the White Elephant casino on the Embankment near Dolphin Square. After this venture failed much of her gear was removed and helped re-rig the sailing barge *C.I.V.*. By this time in a poor way, she was towed to the Blackwater and 'abandoned' in a sinking condition in Maylandsea Creek. *Pretoria's* final resting place is at Promenade Creek near Maldon where her burned out bottom lays in the mud. It is understood that her transom has been preserved ashore.

Esther was built by Alfred Marconi White at the North Brents Yard, Faversham in 1900 for the local firm of Seager. She was registered at Faversham, Official Number 104945. She quickly changed hands being bought by the brick making firm of Horsford and then passed to Cremer for most of her working life.

Esther's master for almost 40 years, both under Horseford and Cremer was Captain Percy Wildish who retired in 1953 after winning the Staysail Class of the Coronation Thames Barge Match. This was no mean feat because the competition in the match was fierce and it was *Esther's* first barge race. This race success provided a fine conclusion to the career of Percy Wildish.

She never defended her win, for when Percy retired in 1953 *Esther* was fitted with an auxiliary engine (unusually mounted on the starboard side) and was soon sold by Cremer to the Whitstable firm of Daniels Brothers. She had her gear removed and traded until 1960 as a motor barge. She ended up as a house barge on the Medway and today her derelict hulk can be seen in West Hoo Creek.

An unusual feature of *Esther* was her very narrow side decks each side of the main hatch. These were modified, it is understood, when Mr Cremer asked each of his masters for suggestions prior to a refit.

Her principle particulars were: Length 80 feet, Beam 19.1 feet, Maximum height under deck 5.5 feet; 43 Reg. Tons, cargo capacity for river work 132 tons.

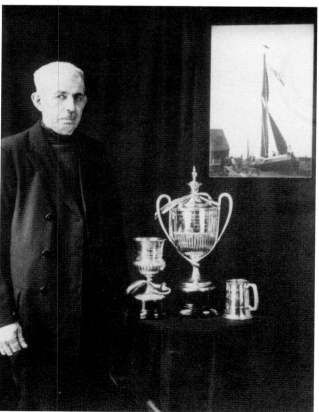

Esther on her way to a class win in the 1953 Coronation Thames Barge Match, with the *Westmoreland* to leeward. The *Westmoreland* sank following stranding at Hoo in 1973, and has lain at Faversham awaiting restoration ever since.

Opposite top: Under sail aboard *Esther*. She is off the wind with the starboard vang slack and the sprit out to port. Smoke from the cabin stove is seen coming from the chimney.

Opposite bottom left: Capt. Percy Wildish seen with his trophies after the 1953 Thames Match, standing by a picture of *Esther* at Hollowshore with her sails set and winner's pennant flying aloft.

Opposite bottom right: By 1954 *Esther* was an auxiliary, sacrificing her mizzen sail for the comfort of a wheelhouse. Shortly after, she was to lose her rig completely, relying on power alone.

James & Ann at Chatham in 1950. The tide has left her well sunk into the soft mud at the berth, as she lies laden with cargo, some stacked above her main hatch coamings.

Opposite bottom: Loaded to her marks, Cremer's Conyer built *James & Ann* carries sawn timber piled high on her hatches and decks during the summer of 1937.

Captain Albert Keen pictured at Ham Wharf in Oare Creek, this photograph taken looking towards the Hollowshore bargeyard.

James & Ann was built at the Conyer yard of Alfred White and was launched in 1903 and registered at Faversham, Official Number 114455. Her original owner was Horsford of Faversham and then Cremer for most of her working life.

She was a very unlucky barge because she was sunk in collision no less than three times, firstly in 1947 and again two years later. Each time she was raised, repaired and put back to work. Later, after Cremer, she was sold away and reduced to a pure motor barge when she was cut down whilst fully loaded off Erith and her master and his wife were drowned.

James & Ann's master both during and after World War II was Captain Albert Keen, who although a very private man, was a good barge master. Like many masters, Albert had his favourite barge and many of his yarns would begin "When I was in the *Violet Sybil*". When he retired from *James & Ann* he was employed for a time as bridge master on Faversham swing bridge.

Her principle particulars were: Length 80 feet, Beam 19.2 feet, Maximum height under deck 5.3 feet; 42 Reg. Tons, cargo capacity for river work 115 tons.

James & Ann's last resting place is not known but it is reasonable to assume that after the fatal accident in November 1952 when the crew were drowned, she was disposed of in the Erith area.

What of Faversham Creek today? It is a mere shadow of what it once was. Although no shipping comes to the crumbling quays, and much of the waterfront is given over to modern housing, Faversham's connections with seaborne trade are not extinct. In 1994 Chris Cook established Faversham Ships Limited. Joined by Nick Sice a few years later, the company has grown to a total of five ships by 2002. Their craft, of around 1,000 - 1,500 Tonnes, include the M.V. *Conformity*, a Dutch built low air draft coaster, now the only cargo carrier registered at Faversham.

There are no craft at all in the Pent above the bridge and the whole Creek is now much silted. A few yachts are berthed in Brents Reach and the south side of the New Cut is home to a number of traditional craft such as sailing barges. The charter barge *Mirosa* is berthed at Iron Wharf and this beautifully maintained barge is one of only two Thames barges not fitted with an engine, the other being the Essex based *Edme*. The entire length of Oare Creek is home to many dozens of yachts.

Seemingly every year there are plans aired about improvements needed to keep the silt from building up and how to make better use of the Creek, but it is very doubtful if anything can be done due to the great cost of such work. One thing, however, that can still be said is that our once commercially vital waterway's legacy is to give enjoyment and safe haven to hundreds of pleasure sailors.

The M.V. *Conformity* is now the only commercial cargo vessel registered at the port of Faversham.

Picture Sources

We are always indebted to all those of our forbears who took the trouble to capture their times and interests on 'film'. The preceding pages are crammed with more than 100 photographs of Faversham and Oare Creeks spanning over 100 years.

The following list indicates many sources, and where possible identifies the photographer and the collection from which the picture has been drawn. Certain photographers warrant special mention. In addition to those whose pictures have appeared in contemporary postcards, there are others whose prolificacy has meant that many have never been seen in print before.

First amongst these must be Frank Crosoer, an amateur photographer like his brother Herbert, he was once manager of what is now the National Westminster Bank in Market Place, Faversham. His pictures, many now in the collection of Faversham historian Peter Kennett, are the oldest included, mostly taken in the late 1800s when he was about 40. His connection with this history is more than just via his camera, for his sister Louisa married Charles Cremer and all were neighbours in Newton Road, Faversham.

Special mention must also be made of the late Richard (Dick) Dadson. Like his father, Dick was born and lived in Faversham and was another keen amateur photographer, particularly capturing the East Swale and it's creeks, and the abundant wild fowl that wintered there or made the area their permanent home. Dick also had the foresight to record interviews with the Faversham bargemen and shipwrights, the latter being his father's calling, a highly skilled occupation which he also took up. Many of his photographs grace these pages, most by kind permission of his widow, Avis Dadson.

Other of these pictures are from the camera or collection of John Cotton, an avid photographer of the Creek and the vessels which visited over many years. Also well represented is the collection of the late Capt. Fred Cooper.

Front Cover: Photograph by Dick Dadson, Avis Dadson collection
Inside Front Cover: Photograph by Dr. Charles Evers, Bob Ratcliffe collection
Title Page Top: Photograph by John Cotton
Title Page Top Centre: Photograph by Roy Dane, Peter Kennett collection
Title Page Bottom Centre: Photograph by Dick Dadson, Peter Kennett collection
Title Page Bottom: Photograph by John Cotton
6: Photograph by Dick Dadson, Avis Dadson collection
7: Faversham Town Council collection
8 Top: Faversham Town Council collection
8 Centre: Faversham Town Council collection
8 Bottom: Aerofilms Limited, John Cotton collection
9 Top and Bottom: Photographs by the author
12: Photograph by Dick Dadson, Avis Dadson collection
13 Top, Centre and Bottom: Photographs by the author
14 Top, Centre and Bottom: Photographs by the author
15: Aerofilms Limited, John Cotton collection
16: Photograph by Frank Crosoer, Peter Kennett collection
17: Photograph by Frank Crosoer, Peter Kennett collection
19 Top: Photograph by Filmer, Peter Kennett collection
19 Bottom: Photograph by the author
20 Top: Photograph by Theo. Barber, Tony Farnham collection
20 Bottom: Photograph by the author
21: Photograph by Dick Dadson, Avis Dadson collection
22 Top and Bottom: Photographs by Dick Dadson, Avis Dadson collection
23: John Cotton collection
24 Top and Bottom: Photographs by Richard Walsh
25: Photograph by the author
26: John Cotton collection
28 Top: Photograph by Frank Crosoer, Peter Kennett collection
28 Bottom: Photograph by Richard-Hugh Perks

30 Top: Photograph by Frank Crosoer, Peter Kennett collection
30 Bottom: Photograph by the author
31 to 37: Photographs by the author
38: John Cotton collection
39: Photograph by Richard-Hugh Perks
40: Barry and Marion Tester collection
41 Top: Photograph by Theo. Barber, Peter Kennett collection
41 Bottom: Peter Kennett collection
42: Faversham Society collection
43: Photograph by Dr. Charles Evers, Bob Ratcliffe collection
44 Top: Photograph by Dr. Charles Evers, Bob Ratcliffe collection
44 Bottom: Photograph by the author
45: Photograph by Frank Crosoer, Peter Kennett collection
46 Top: Photograph by Dick Dadson, Avis Dadson collection
46 Bottom: Photograph by the author
47 Top: Photograph by Dick Dadson, Avis Dadson collection
47 Bottom: Photograph by Richard-Hugh Perks
48 Top: Photograph by Dick Dadson, Avis Dadson collection
48 Bottom: Photograph by Richard-Hugh Perks
49 Top: Photograph by Richard-Hugh Perks
49 Bottom: Photograph by Frank Crosoer, Peter Kennett collection
50: Photograph by Frank Crosoer, Peter Kennett collection
51 Top: Photograph by William Hargrave, Peter Kennett collection
51 Bottom: Photograph by Dick Dadson, Avis Dadson collection
52 Top: Photograph by Richard Walsh
52 Bottom: Photograph by Dr. Charles Evers, Bob Ratcliffe collection
53: Photograph by Frank Crosoer, Peter Kennett collection
54 Top: Photograph by Frank Crosoer, Peter Kennett collection
54 Bottom: Photograph by Richard-Hugh Perks
55 Top: Photograph by Dick Dadson, Avis Dadson collection
55 Bottom: Photograph by John Cotton
56 Top and Bottom: Photographs by Dick Dadson, John Cotton collection
57 Top: Photograph by Frank Crosoer, Peter Kennett collection
57 Bottom: Valentine & Sons Limited post card, John Cotton collection
58 Top and Bottom: Photographs by John Cotton
59 Top: Photograph by William Hargrave from post card, Gary Vaughan collection
59 Bottom: Photograph by Frank Crosoer, Peter Kennett collection
60 Top and Bottom: Photographs by John Cotton
61 Top: John Cotton collection
61 Bottom: Photograph by Dr. Charles Evers, Bob Ratcliffe collection
62: Taylors, Eastbourne post card, John Cotton collection
64: Photograph by Richard Walsh
65: Photograph by Theo. Barber, Peter Kennett collection
66 Top: Photograph by T.C. Hart, ex. Fred Cooper collection, Ray Rush collection
66 Bottom: Ex. Fred Cooper collection, Ray Rush collection
67 Top and Bottom: Photographs by Dr. Charles Evers, Bob Ratcliffe collection
68: National Maritime Museum, London
69 Top: John Cotton collection
69 Bottom: Ex. Fred Cooper collection, Ray Rush collection
70: National Maritime Museum, London
71 Top: John Cotton collection
71 Bottom: Photograph by The Times
72 Top Left: John Cotton collection
72 Bottom Left: Wildish Family collection
72 Bottom Right: Ex. Fred Cooper collection, Ray Rush collection
73: Ex. Fred Cooper collection, Ray Rush collection
74: Ex. Fred Cooper collection, Ray Rush collection
75 Top: Keen Family collection
75 Bottom: Photograph by R. Stimpson Jnr., ex. Fred Cooper collection, Ray Rush collection
76: Faversham Ships Limited
Inside Back Cover: Ex. Fred Cooper collection, Ray Rush collection
Back Cover: Photograph by Dick Dadson, Avis Dadson collection

East Swale Jetty and Dock Plans

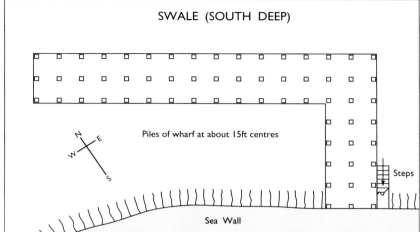

SWALE (SOUTH DEEP)

Piles of wharf at about 15ft centres

Steps

Sea Wall

The explosives jetty just to the west of Stinket Ness (see p.13)

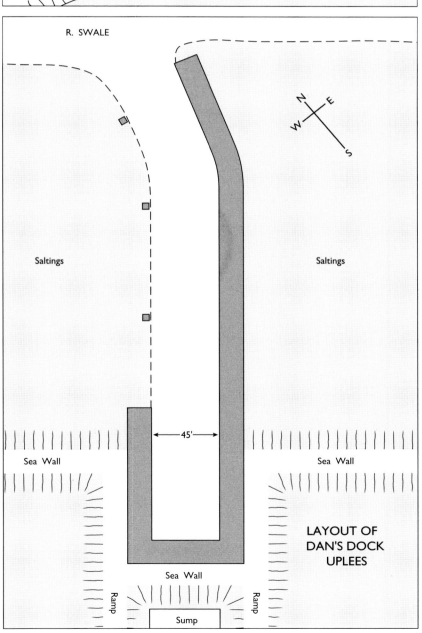

R. SWALE

Saltings

Saltings

←45'→

Sea Wall

Sea Wall

Sea Wall

LAYOUT OF DAN'S DOCK UPLEES

Ramp

Ramp

Sump

Dan's Dock at Uplees (see p.14)

Index

Names of vessels are shown in *italics* and figures in bold refer to plates.

Index prepared by Jane Gilbert
of
Indexing Specialists
202 Church Road
Hove
East Sussex BN3 2DJ

Jane Gilbert was at one time
a resident of Faversham.